GRAND SLAM!

By PETE ALFANO

GRAND SLAM

FIRST PRINTING . . . FEBRUARY, 1973

Library of Congress Card Number 73-75001

Photo Credits: Dan Rubin, U.P.I. Photo, Bill Mark

Crowd reaction tells the story as Tony Jacklin sinks a long putt.

TABLE OF CONTENTS

GOLF'S GRAND SLAM

. . . THE CHALLENGE IS THERE

■ The challenge has always been there . . . in every sport.

It is there in the common desire of super athletes to scale the heights of achievement and to establish new standards of excellence. It is there in the inner drive, the motivation, that lifts one competitor above his contemporaries.

For some men, winning alone is not enough. They are driven beyond the goal of winning. These men are the true super-stars of professional sports. They are the men whose mere presence dominates a game or a tournament or a season. Jack Nicklaus is such a man. So is Joe Namath. Wilt Chamberlain is another. They, and others like them, tower over their fellow athletes, not in physical size but in accomplishment.

It is not just money that motivates these great performers. Nor do they seek only fame and recognition. No, it is something else, something more subtle, a feeling beyond the understanding of men who have never tempered their minds and bodies in the white-hot fires of big-time competition. It is one man's desire to excel—not for the benefit of anyone else, but for himself, for the pure inner satisfaction that excellence brings to a proud and dedicated professional.

Success alone does not always answer this need. The truly great ones consider success in their chosen profession as only the first step along the road to loftier achievement. Success, to them, is doing something no one else has ever done—or that only a few men have ever done. Success is measured not in lines in the record book or in a Hall of Fame niche. It is measured, for these superstars, in being the very best. It is measured in attaining the unattainable goal.

In track and field, it was the four-minute mile barrier, then the 70-foot shot put and finally the 18-foot pole vault. In baseball it was Babe Ruth's record of 60 home runs (eventually surpassed by Roger Maris of the Yankees in 1961). In horse racing it is sweeping the famed Triple Crown—the Kentucky Derby, The Preakness and The Belmont Stakes. In tennis it is the Big Four of the French, Australian and U.S. titles plus Wimbledon.

And in professional golf it's the

legendary Grand Slam—The Masters, the British and U.S. Opens and the PGA.

Over the years, golf's Grand Slam has truly been one of the most elusive of all goals in sports. The incomparable Bobby Jones achieved the first Grand Slam back in 1930. Since then, however, it has defied the game's greatest competitors, the Ben Hogans, the Sam Sneads, the Arnold Palmers. It has remained tantalizingly beyond the reach of the finest players of each succeeding era. It has been the pot of gold at the end of golf's rainbow. It is the one thing the game's superstars covet the most.

From the very beginning it was felt that if any one man had the talent, the skill, the dedication to emulate Jones' Grand Slam triumph, that man was Jack Nicklaus. Well, in 1972, Nicklaus got his chance. He made his run at the four major titles—with the whole world rooting for him—and he failed. He captured The Masters at Augusta, the first leg of the Slam, and then picked up additional momentum with a stirring triumph in the U.S. Open. He was halfway there when he left to play in the British Open.

It was in there that Jack saw his Grand Slam bid fade before his eyes, and it was fellow American pro Lee Trevino, Nicklaus' most persistent challenger, who did him in. Lee made a miraculous chip shot on the back nine of the final round to snatch the British Open title from Nicklaus' grasp—and end, at least for another year, Big Jack's chance of equaling Bobby Jones' legendary feat.

Nicklaus earned over $300,000 on the pro tour in 1972, the first golfer ever to surpass that magical plateau, but it's safe to say that Jack might have settled for a lot less had he been able to add the Grand Slam to his amazing list of achievements. "You reach a point," explains golf's golden boy, "when achievement means more than dollars and cents."

But Jack Nicklaus will be back in quest of the elusive Grand Slam again, and so will the others with the ability and the perseverance to capture the world's four major golf titles, men like Trevino and Player, Casper and Palmer, Sanders and Crampton, and all the other fine shot-makers who follow the sun—and the big cash payoffs—on the professional tour.

Some day one of these great players, or maybe it will be one of the promising youngsters on the tour, will put it all together in one big year and win the Grand Slam. The drives will boom straight down the fairways, the iron shots will whistle unerringly to the pin and the long putts will take the break and drop into the cup. That's what it will take to win the Grand Slam. It will take golfing skill, physical stamina, mental application. It will take lots of luck and perhaps a sprinkling of magic.

Yes, some day it will be done again. Someone's name will go up there next to that of Bobby Jones, and golf will have two Grand Slam heroes. In the meantime, the chase continues, adding color and excitement and another dimension to the game of golf.

That's what this book is all about . . . . ■

The legendary Bobby Jones poses with his Grand Slam trophies in 1930.

BOBBY JONES: 'HE WAS PERFECTION'

■ Since the day in 1488 when James the IV of Scotland climbed down from his throne long enough to play nine holes before lunch and thereby make it possible for his countrymen to be remembered for something more than their distinctive brand of whiskey, few have had as much success chasing the elusive white golf ball as the late Bobby Jones.

Bobby was born in Atlanta, Georgia, and by the age of five he was following his parents around the East Lake Country Club course, through alternating weeds and woods, small bodies of shallow water and kidney-shaped dust bowls, all man-made obstacles leading to the well-manicured lawn where lay the small round cup and the end of a journey which started several hundred yards earlier. It was no wonder that in his youth Bobby Jones was to tell his father, "I like fishing and baseball better. Golf's too slow."

But his lawyer-father suspected the natural talents for the game his son displayed and helped to foster them. Much of what Bobby learned was through observation and the rest was through the tutoring of Stewart Maiden, a smooth-swinging Scot from Carnoustie, whose style was easy to follow. By the age of nine, Bobby Jones won the junior championship cup of the Atlanta Athletic Club. By 13, he qualified in the Southern Amateur but lost in the second round. And a year later, in 1916, the chubby youngster in the white knickers played in his first U.S. Amateur championship.

Playing against men almost twice his age, Bobby won two rounds of match play before losing to Bob Gardner, 4 and 3, in the third round. It would only be a matter of time, however, before Jones would rule the game of golf. And it was in 1930 that he accomplished what no other golfer had done previously or since. Bobby Jones won the Grand Slam as he methodically clubbed his way to victory in the U.S. Amateur, the U.S. Open, the British Amateur and the British Open.

It ranks with the greatest sports feats of all time. It was Babe Ruth hitting 60 home runs and Gertrude Ederle swimming the English Channel. It was, perhaps, more. Although he had already won nine major championships, no one had expected him to completely dominate his fellow golfers and the well-conceived courses that were designed to test man to the limits of his physical and mental abilities. But Bobby Jones was a rarity. He sought perfection and it was evident in his accurate drives and flawless putts. It was a style even James the IV of Scotland could have appreciated.

Although the origin of golf has been fixed in Scotland, the exact time of its birth is more difficult to pin down. There are some historians who believe some primitive forms of the game were played in various other parts of the world. It was known, however, that James the II of Scotland prohibited the game in 1440, claiming it took up too much leisure time. It's a theory many modern day housewives would gladly agree with when their husbands spend all day Saturday at the nearest country club or public course.

James the II wasn't worrying about the lawn that needed cutting or the paint that was peeling in the living room. He thought golf kept his subjects from learning the art of bow and arrow warfare. However, James the IV and James the V were more enlightened. So was Mary Queen of Scots, a duffer of sorts herself in the early and mid 1500s.

By 1552, a 6,883-yard course was built in Scotland and it was called St. Andrews, to this day the most famous golf course in the world. It is one that every established pro golfer and every bright-eyed young amateur wants to play. And following the construction of St. Andrews, golf clubs emerged—the most famous of which is the Royal and Ancient Golf Club which was established in 1754.

Men played for belts then and not the huge purses that have made millionaires of today's golfers. Their clubs had hickory shafts and the early golf ball was made of feathers stuffed inside a leather cover. The distance it traveled depended on how tightly the feathers were stuffed and the average range was from 175 to 200 yards. By the late 1800s, the rubber golf ball was introduced in the United States and used at courses such as the Foxburg Golf Club in Pennsylvania, established in 1887 and believed to be the oldest in the country.

So the pioneer work had been done and along came the men to challenge each other and the courses. Some dominated, and their names are synonymous with golf. They are men such as Gene Sarazen, Harry Vardon, Ted Ray and Walter Hagen. And there was Walter J. Travis, a man who at 35 won the first tournament he ever entered in 1915 just a month after he hit his first golf ball.

But as formidable as some of the early golfers were, they were all to take a back seat to Bobby Jones. And the long-awaited moment arrived in 1923 at the Inwood course on Long Island when he won the U.S. Open championship at the age of 21. Jones shot rounds of 71, 73 and 76, which gave him a three-stroke lead entering the final round. His closest challenger was Bobby Cruickshank, a name as difficult to pronounce as it was so simple to say Bobby Jones. And Jones played steady golf that final day, needing only a par 4 on the troublesome 425-yard 18th hole to win the tournament.

Gene Sarazen won most of golf's major titles in 1920s and 1930s.

Hagen had predicted Jones would win the Open before winning the Amateur and now Bobby was just a few shots from making

Francis Ouimet (center) beat Henry Vardon (L) and Ted Ray in 1913 Open.

Hagen a prophet. With the wind blowing slightly against him, Jones hit a good drive off the tee, but his second shot hooked into the rough. Then he found a bunker and when he finally hit the green, his lead was in jeopardy. He took a six on the 18th hole and finished with 296. As Jones waited, Cruickshank, an unflappable Scotsman, took advantage of the unexpected collapse and came back to tie Jones. A playoff was set for the next day.

"I didn't finish like a champion," Jones said. "I finished like a yellow dog."

By the following day, Jones had regained his confidence and held a two-stroke advantage at the 13th hole. Cruickshank came back again, picking up one hole at the 14th and the other at the 15th. Jones held firm and they came to the final hole all even. The day before it had been his undoing, but now Bobby Jones challenged the 18th at Inwood and, on his second shot, sent the ball to within six feet of the cup. Moments later he had won the Open and the era of Bobby Jones had begun.

In 1924 Bobby won the U.S.

Amateur, defeating George Von Elm, 9 and 8, in the final match. He was also a member of the United States Walker Cup team. In 1925 he won the Amateur again and in 1926 at the age of 24, Jones spread his fame overseas. He won the British Open at St. Anne's with a 72-hole total of 291. He also won the U.S. Open and won both of his Walker Cup matches.

His mastery continued in 1927 as he won the U.S. Amateur and the British Open. And it continued the following two years as he dominated the Walker Cup matches and took down another U.S. Amateur and Open title. By 1930, his place in golf's Hall of Fame was already assured. But little did anyone know that this would be his greatest year ever. At 28, there seemed little left for him to conquer. And there were those who urged him to turn pro and reap the monetary benefits. Instead, he remained an amateur and, fittingly, his Grand Slam bid began at St. Andrews in Scotland.

Jones was anything but perfection during the early rounds, but St. Andrews had been known to make hackers of the best golfers. He gained the final nonetheless and defeated Roger Wethered, 7 and 6. There was a crowd of 25,000 watching with more than the usual reserve for which the British are noted. The people embraced him as he left the course and headed for the clubhouse, and the tired young man was given a police escort. He further won the spectators' respect and accolades when he paid the homeland of golf and weather-beaten St. Andrews the ultimate tribute.

"I would have rather won this tournament than any other in the world," he said.

From St. Andrews, Jones followed his destiny to Hoylake and the British Open. Again he struggled, though this time it was in the closing rounds. He shot a 70 and 72 the first two days and seemed about to run off with the title. On the third day, however, he faltered and shot a 74. Perhaps the pressure was beginning to build because, on the final day, Jones shot his poorest round—a 75.

He had started early and was forced to await the outcome in the clubhouse. Ironically, it wasn't the British who challenged his lead; it was two Americans. Leo Diegel and MacDonald Smith charged furiously at Jones' 291 total, but both fell short at 293. Jones had triumphed over Britain, and the boy from the colonies returned to a hero's welcome.

But it would be his countrymen who would help add to the already-mounting pressure. Newspaper accounts told of his exploits in Britain and asked whether he could continue his dominance in the States. The Grand Slam was the topic of conversation and people questioned whether the young Jones could hold up under the pressure. His courage as well as his game would be tested at the Interlochen golf course in Minneapolis, site of the U.S. Open.

The best in American and European golf would be taking part. It was the 34th Open, but perhaps the best publicized. The public sensed history in the making and knew Bobby Jones would have his hands full with the likes of Tommy Armour, Harry Cooper, Johnny Farrell, Craig Wood, Horton Smith and MacDonald Smith, a name Jones had learned well as he nervously waited for the outcome at Hoylake. It was a tournament of champions and, above all, a test of a man against nature. Jones would not only have to defeat a star-studded field, he would also have to take the measure of Interlochen.

After a first-round 71, Jones trailed MacDonald Smith and Tommy Armour. And after the second round, Bobby knew he wasn't going to run away from this field. He shot a 73 and fell further back as Horton Smith fired a 70 for a two-round total of 142, two strokes better than Jones. Harry Cooper, famous in earlier years for his charges from behind, was tied with Jones. Bobby was still favored, but it seemed the odds against him were beginning to mount.

And then Jones played the game of golf as he had never done in the past. Perhaps he had shot better rounds, but never under the pressure that faced him in Minneapolis. Bobby Jones didn't need the sympathy of the spectators; he didn't need America's support as its sentimental choice. The sympathy should have been saved for his competition.

Jones fired a 68 on the third round, five strokes better than anyone else. It wasn't the young man whose arms stiffened and whose putter wavered. It was the veterans, golfers like MacDonald Smith, who shot a 74, and Harry Cooper, who came in with a 75. Then there was Horton Smith's 76 and Tommy Armour's 75. Only one other golfer was to play a round in the 60s in the 1930 Open and he was a little-known pro from California named Monte Dutra, who somehow shot a 69 while running up scores of 76, 78 and 80 in the other rounds.

By the final day of the tournament, the talk was whether Bobby Jones would win the last leg of the Slam, the National Amateur. What occurred at Interlochen was anti-climactic. Jones allowed himself the luxury of relaxing on that final day and his score soared to 75. He knew he had won and the superb concentration he had displayed earlier over every shot was missing. Perhaps it was his youth that was betraying him, but people were probably relieved to know he was human, after all. MacDonald Smith gave one last futile try but the margin was too big. Smith finished with a 70, still two strokes behind Jones' winning total of 287. Bobby Jones had won the U.S. Open. If he thought the pressure was almost too much to bear up to that point, surely it would be doubled at Merion, Pennsylvania, site of the U.S. Amateur. But Bobby ventured forth.

If Bobby Jones felt that pressure, however, it wasn't evident in his style. In fact, it seemed as if the only nervous ones were his opponents and the spectators when the 34th Amateur began on September 22 at the suburban golf course just outside Philadelphia. If Bobby Jones was awed by what lay before him, he was the last one to let it show.

Unlike the medal play of the previous two tournaments, the Amateur consisted of match play and head-to-head confrontations. Jones' first opponent was Ross Somerville, a Canadian. It was a morning match and Jones barely broke a sweat as he beat his opponent, 5 and four. After lunch he faced another Canadian in Fred Hoblitzel and the match was a repeat of his morning activities. Jones won, 5 and 4, and it was evident no one in Canada was going to deprive him of the Grand Slam.

If it could be believed with all that was at stake, the next two matches were easier. Jones rose to the task as he easily defeated Fay Coleman of California, 6 and 5, and then turned his machine-like game on former Walker Cup teammate Jess Sweetser who fell victim, 9 and 8. Jones had gained the final round and was 36 holes away from golf history.

On the final day his opponent was Gene Homans of the Englewood, N.J., Country Club. And though Homans was a veteran golfer, he was no match for the man "with the perfect swing." Jones defeated Homans, 8 and 7, to win the Amateur championship and Golf's Grand Slam.

If some thought Bobby Jones had attained all he could possibly desire before 1930, there was now little doubt there were no worlds left for him to conquer. He could turn pro and use his talent to make himself a rich man. At 28, Jones had many profitable years ahead of him. But he chose to retire instead, just a few short months after he won the Amateur. He was at the top of his game and some would have considered it stealing had Jones decided to play for money.

He left the tour to make instructional movies and to run the Masters Tournament which has replaced the U.S. Amateur as one of the tournaments in the modern-day Grand Slam. Bobby Jones had been motivated by his love of the game. He had been driven by his desire for perfection and to be the best. To idealists, Jones was a hero, a man unmoved by the monetary rewards of winning golf tournaments. It's why others speak of him with unlimited respect.

"He was absolutely perfect," declared Francis Ouimet. "It was discouraging and monotonous the way he hit practically every shot as it should be hit. If he had come along 15 or 20 years later, he still would have been the best."

Walter Hagen thought Jones had already achieved that distinction.

"If I were asked to vote for the greatest golfer of all time I'd have to mark my ballot for Bobby Jones," Hagen said.

In 1926 Bobby was given a ticker-tape parade down the caverns of Broadway in New York City after he had won the U.S. Open. His retirement was less flamboyant and he admitted the pressure of winning the Grand Slam had taken something out of golf for him.

"It just wasn't fun any longer," he said. "In the beginning nothing much was expected of me and I enjoyed battling the older fellows.

I enjoyed the challenge of beating, or attempting to beat, the top players of the day. But as I began winning, and as more and more was expected of me, I found the pressure distasteful.

"It was no longer fun, and I had always played golf for the fun of it," he added. "When it got to be 1925 and golf became a serious business for me, I was expected to win or finish well up in every tournament I entered. After the big year (1930), I decided I had had enough. I chose the easier and more gracious way in non-competitive golf."

Some of the older fellows Bobby Jones enjoyed competing against in golf's early years were men like Walter Hagen and Gene Sarazen. Both were colorful players who attracted huge followings as they went from one tournament to another. Hagen was brash and confident and backed his words with success on the course. He won the U.S. Open in 1914 and 1919; the British Open in 1922, 1924, 1928 and 1929 and took the PGA championship in 1921 and then won it from 1924 through 1927. He also won many other tournaments, including the French and Canadian Opens, and was captain of the Ryder Cup team six times.

While he was a great showman, Hagen was also a fine shotmaker. He became a full-time caddie at the age of 12 in Rochester, N.Y., and learned his golf by watching and imitating the style of others. He turned pro at 19. He was an

Gravely ill Bobby Jones congratulates Gary Player after 1961 Masters win.

expert in the sand at a time before the sand-wedge had been invented. He didn't waste time pondering his shots; he walked up and struck the ball as if his approach was part of his swing.

Of Hagen it has been written, "he makes more bad shots in a single season than Harry Vardon did during the whole period of 1890-1914 . . . but he beats more immaculate golfers because three of 'those' and one of 'them' count four, and he knows it."

Gene Sarazen had his triumphs too, including the U.S. Open in 1922 and 1932; the British Open in 1932 and the PGA in 1922, 1923 and 1933. He also won the Masters in 1935 and the Seniors title in 1954 and 1958. Yet, he's a man who has said: "No golfer could achieve greatness unless he had experienced hunger." Sometimes he failed to finish a tournament in his early years because of a lack of money. It was a situation remedied by his ability with a golf club.

He was stocky, with strong arms and a personality that enabled him to endure the good and bad. At 20, he went from unknown to a household word when he won the U.S. Open and the Professional Golfers Association (PGA) titles. He went to Troon, full of confidence in his ability to add the British Open to his collection, but he failed to qualify by a stroke. "I'll come back," he promised. And in 1932, he finally won the British Open.

Harry Vardon was the pioneer of golf at the turn of the century, a young gardener in the English island of Jersey who turned professional at a time when Americans had yet to make their first golf course. In 1900 Vardon made a tour of the United States and everywhere he went, the game of golf gained popularity. His swing, his style and his theories were widely copied. In all parts of the country, this three-time winner of the British Open found people eager to learn his methods. He gave demonstrations and played exhibition matches, and soon many were using his grip and imitating his swing. His influence continued until the outbreak of World War I, which marked the end of the Vardon era.

Perhaps more for his teachings than his playing, few golfers are accorded as much respect as Tommy Armour, another of the early golfers. He was born in Edinburgh in 1896 and the young Scotsman took to the golf clubs as American children take to a baseball bat. After gaining experience in his own country, Armour came to the U.S. in 1924 where he turned professional. He won the U.S. Open in 1927 and, in the years following, he took the PGA and British Open titles. Tommy was tall and slim, a man whose power came from a whiplash swing and a delicate sense of timing. He was one who believed that the outstanding golfers were also outstanding athletes.

It took golfers such as Vardon, Hagen, Sarazen and Armour to lay the groundwork. They introduced Americans to the game of golf and helped it out of its infancy. But it was Bobby Jones who gave golf its biggest boost when he completed the Grand Slam in 1930. ■

JACK NICKLAUS: ONLY ONE HORIZON LEFT TO CONQUER

■ The sun-bleached blond hair falls uncombed over his forehead and when he speaks it's in the high-pitched tones of a choir boy. But from the tips of his spike shoes to the top of his backswing, Jack Nicklaus is a source of power that has dominated golf from the day he turned pro in 1962 and won the first tournament he entered—the U.S. Open. Golf may be a game for others. For Nicklaus, it's child's play.

At 32, Jack Nicklaus is a millionaire several times over.

Determination is etched on Jack Nicklaus' face as he strides onto green at Westchester.

Born in Columbus, Ohio in 1940, he somehow managed to grow up in the traditional football region with a golf club in his hands instead of a helmet on his head. He attended Ohio State and played on the golf team, not one of Woody Hayes' football powers. He has the build of a guard—compact, with muscular arms, shoulders and thighs. As a young pro he also had an extra pound or two around the middle and he was called "Fat Jack." In recent years he has trimmed some of the fat but still retains the power that makes him the game's longest hitter. A golf club is like a spoon in his hands.

Rarely had a golfer burst upon the scene with as much fanfare as Nicklaus. He had won the U.S. Amateur two out of three years when he turned pro and observers compared him to Bobby Jones, Nicklaus' boyhood idol. Even at 22, he was a cool master of his own game—a player who remained unruffled from tee to green. He is a perfectionist; a man whose game is under careful scrutiny from himself.

"The golf swing for me is a source of never-ending fascination," Jack says. "On the one hand, the swings of all the outstanding golfers are decidedly individual but, on the other hand, the champions all execute approximately the same moves at the critical stages of the swing. There is still a lot about the swing we don't know and probably never will. In any event, scarcely a day goes by when I don't find myself thinking about the golf swing."

Nicklaus is a machine, much as Jones was considered a mechanical man when he dominated golf. But Jones played in near privacy compared to Nicklaus. Jones' audiences were the galleries. For Nicklaus the galleries are larger and there are millions more watching on television. The coverage by the media has increased largely because Jones was an amateur who would not earn a dime from his victory, while Nicklaus takes home anywhere from $20,000 to $50,000 per victory. And victories in the more prestigious tournaments often result in lucrative side benefits in endorsements. Jones played for love; Nicklaus plays for love and money.

The galleries demand more from Nicklaus than near perfection. After all they had been introduced to golf by Arnold Palmer, the sport's first pin-up boy. The fans seemed to enjoy watching Palmer make his million. They seemed to resent the colorless Nicklaus. Arnie would struggle, then charge from behind in spectacular fashion. His trials were clearly evident by the expressions on his face—the grimmace, pain and bright smile. Nicklaus kept his emotions to himself and never let them get the best of him. So while his legions were large, they never equaled Arnie's Army in the early years.

The years have produced a compromise. Television has made the golfer a show business personality and a performer. Nicklaus

Powerful Arnold Palmer has long been arch-rival of Nicklaus—and close friend, too.

has sensed it and is now more outgoing and demonstrative on the course. And the galleries have come to appreciate him for himself. No longer do they ask Jack to compete with Palmer for the title of "Mr. Congeniality."

But the pressure on Nicklaus to win is still great. Despite the increasing number of golfers who can win any given tournament, it is considered a mild upset when Jack doesn't win the ones he enters. At one time, five years ago, people wondered out loud whether he had lost his competitive edge. He was rich and he had won all the major tournaments. He regularly earned over $100,000 in prize winnings, and in the last three years, has taken down over $200,000. In 1972, he finally topped the $300,000 barrier. What was there left for Nicklaus to conquer?

The answer wasn't that difficult. It's posed every now and then, although those who ask the question realize there are few golfers capable of attaining the Grand Slam. Since Bobby Jones became the first golfer to complete the Slam in 1930, no one has come close. Not Palmer, Gary Player or Billy Casper in recent years, or Ben Hogan and Sam Snead in the 1940s and 1950s. Not even Nicklaus.

For some reason 1972 was chosen as the year Nicklaus would make the challenge. It wasn't Jack who encouraged the talk; he said the odds against it were "one million to one." That was before the Masters Tournament in Augusta, Ga., the first leg of the modern Slam. Since the monetary rewards are too important now, rarely does a golfer remain an amateur for very long. Thus, the U.S. and British Amateurs have lost much of their luster and have been replaced by the Masters and Professional Golfers' Association (PGA) tournament as part of the Grand Slam. The other two tournaments remain the same. The U.S. Open and the British Open.

Thus, the quest began in April, in the spring, the season that

Sam Snead, now 60, couldn't keep pace with Jack in 1972 Masters.

seems best suited to begin the year. Yet golfers had been playing for huge purses since January when the year-long tour began. Then they ventured to California and Florida, the warm-weather spots and the celebrity tournaments. The year was young and though each tournament was serious business, the bigger names on the tour seemed to enjoy breaking par with the likes of Andy Williams, Jackie Gleason and Bob Hope. The Grand Slam would come later.

And as is the case every January, the new faces made their presence felt. The list seemed to grow each year. Last year the newcomers included Grier Jones, Jerry Heard, Mike Hill, Lanny Wadkins and others. Some, like Wadkins, making their first tour, and others finally achieving a measure of success after several years of trying. Soon, it seemed, it would be impossible to win the Slam. No longer were there just one or two golfers to beat. Now every week brought a serious challenge from a mod-haired kid just a few years out of college.

Still, Jack Nicklaus was supposed to win the Masters. His strength would be an advantage on a course where there were many hills and valleys. A Nicklaus drive could avoid most of them. And with 11 major championships to his credit, he needed just two to tie Jones for the most. No one would forgive Jack for losing and ruining the drama that would build on his search for the Grand Slam.

Nicklaus didn't let them down at Augusta. Though the greens were dreadful and the course played poorly, Jack fashioned an opening round 68 and led the field all the way to win with a total of 286. Only three others broke 290 and one was Jim Jamieson, a chubby young pro from Illinois—the kind of newcomer Nicklaus would have to watch.

Even Sam Snead, now 60 years old, an age when most are enjoying retirement, shot a 69 on the first day. He would not be in the chase for long, however. Nicklaus played well, though only his driver was working in the typical Nicklaus style. He kept his cool as always, but now and then smiled and joked with the gallery about his misfortunes.

"Trying to play safe is the worst thing in the world," he says. "I don't think I would have looked so bad if I'd been forced to throw the ball into the hole."

If there was one source of irritation, however, it was the constant reminder of the Grand Slam.

"You come here to savor the Masters," he said. "It stands alone. I don't think about winning the Masters as part of the Slam. You want to win the Masters because of what it means to the game; what Bob Jones meant."

And so, it wasn't unusual to find Nicklaus on the practice tee hours after he had completed a round. If he were alive, Jones would have understood. Merely leading the field wasn't good enough for Nicklaus, not if his own game was below par.

"I've played better here and didn't win, but the course changes and the field changes," he said.

The field had one newcomer, although Lee Trevino was no stranger to the tour. The year before he won the U.S., British and Canadian Opens and became Nicklaus' most formidable opponent. Now, as if fate had decided to put as much pressure on Nicklaus as possible, Trevino decided to enter the Masters for the first time. He avoided it in past years because he said the course was not suited to his game. Many thought his reason went deeper than that, but Lee proved in 1972 that Augusta was not for him. He never challenged.

Arnold Palmer still had his Army, but the man who once "owned" the Masters also was never in contention. After that opening 68, Nicklaus finished with unspectacular rounds of 71-73-74 to win his fourth Masters, tying him with Palmer as the only other four-time winner. With the victories came the traditional green coat. Only one came easily, and that was in 1963, when he shot 271 and won by nine strokes. But there were those who thought this one was difficult only because Jack made it that way. Perhaps the talk of the Grand Slam was getting to him. Like it or not, he had won the first leg and the pressure and talk would only increase.

There were two months between the Masters and U.S. Open and Nicklaus did not rest. He kept his game sharp through competition. He would have to be at his best for the Open. The tournament was being held at Pebble Beach, Calif., on one of the three courses the golfers play the Bing Crosby National-Pro Amateur. Memories of Pebble Beach usually aren't pleasant ones. It's a course one journalist called "double bogey by the sea." Again it seemed as if everything was being made as difficult as possible for Nicklaus. If indeed, he was to win the Slam, it would not come easy. Pebble Beach, where if the wind don't getcha, the ocean will. Cold, damp and foreboding. If anyone should be favored in the Open, it's the course itself. No one's game could look good at Pebble Beach, not even Bobby Jones, who lost in the first round of the U.S. Amateur there in 1947. Jack Nicklaus had a little better luck; he won the Amateur on the same course in 1961. But this was different. This was the second stop on the way to the Grand Slam and bringing a record 13 holes of the tournament into the living rooms of the viewing public would make the tournament a household word by Sunday night.

Playing Pebble Beach is for a golfer, something similiar to holding the seventh game of the World Series on a sandlot field, complete with broken bottles, rocks and uneven grass. Pebble Beach is tough and the beauty lies in the setting, not in its greens, fairways or traps. More than one golfer would be rolling up his trouser legs and walking by the water's edge to play his next shot. More than one would be tempted to continue walking until the cold

Gary Player joined Nicklaus and Palmer to form golf's "Big Three."

waters of the Pacific closed over his head. Welcome to Pebble Beach.

Twenty-two television cameras and thousands of fans in the galleries were there on the last weekend in June to witness the undoing of every big and small-name golfer in the country. Men sitting at home and sipping on a beer could smile as professionals trudged around the course like weekend hackers at a local golf club. No mercy had Pebble Beach for anyone, not Arnold Palmer, Lee Trevino, Frank Beard or even Jack Nicklaus. But someone had to win and Nicklaus withstood the indignity best of all. He won with a total of 290, which really means Pebble Beach won. But Nicklaus had his Open—and one half of the Grand Slam.

It was the 72nd Open and most of the scores were well above that. George Archer, a competent and steady pro, shot 87 one day. Beard came in with an 85. Nicklaus had a 74 on the final day, when a gale-force wind pushed the scores even higher. And it was under those conditions that Nicklaus also notched his 13th major title—tying him with Jones. It included three U.S. Opens, four Masters, two British Opens and two PGA championships. And in winning the Masters and Open in 1972, he led or shared the lead in every round.

"From now on, Jack is going to have trouble even breathing," Arnold Palmer said after the Open.

After Thursday, the opening round, Nicklaus was tied with five others for the lead. He was part of a five-way tie again on Friday and only Kermit Zarley was included from opening day. By Saturday, Nicklaus moved out to a minimal, but well-appreciated, one-stroke lead. And, behold, in the distance, wasn't that Arnold Palmer and Lee Trevino making a bid? It was.

So on Sunday, it was everything the ABC-TV cameras had hoped it would be. The course was making it rough on the golfers and the golfers were making it rough on each other. What a way to finish a tournament, with Trevino, Palmer and Nicklaus strutting down the fairways. Trevino was his joking self and Nicklaus was confident.

"The only thing I'm going to throw at these guys today is my golf game," he said.

After seven holes, he had increased his slim lead to two strokes and was playing steady golf. At the 10th hole his lead was up to four strokes and it looked like a rout. But Pebble Beach had not overlooked Nicklaus; the monster course was merely biding its time. On the 10th tee, Jack drove into the ocean. He teed up another ball and sent it to the edge of a cliff. When he finished the hole, he had a double bogey. At the 12th hole his tee shot went bounding past the green, down a hill and into the rough. He settled for a bogey.

"I went to bed Saturday night thinking I had to shoot at least a 70 to win," he said. "But this morning when I saw the first green and the wind, I knew it would be a tough son of a gun. I'd have to have patience."

With Palmer and Bruce Cramp-

Bruce Crampton has been one of top foreign players on U.S. tour.

ton still in contention, Nicklaus saved the victory and his chance for the Slam on the 17th hole. It was a par three normally, but in the gale Jack would be lucky to avoid another bogey. He hit an iron and the ball knifed through the wind, avoided a bunker and nestled just two inches from the cup. The Open belonged to Nicklaus.

Four days of wind, sand and the Pacific Ocean had failed to get the best of Nicklaus. More than ever he seemed invincible, the man who could win any tournament he put his mind to. And if Jack Nicklaus had put his mind to winning the Grand Slam, who was going to stop him? Next on the list was the British Open at Muirfield, Scotland. The pressure would build even more, and he would have an added disadvantage of competing in a foreign country. If anyone could do it, however, "Fat Jack" was the man! Although he had won two British Opens, Nicklaus had not always done well in Scotland. He had competed every year since 1963 and won his first at Muirfield in 1966. Never, however, was there the added pressure of trying to win the Grand Slam.

"I try to look at it realistically," he said. "I'll take them as they come, one at a time."

Arnold Palmer held the Masters and U.S. Open titles when he lost the British Open by one stroke at famous St. Andrews in 1960. With that in mind, Jack came to Muirfield early to prepare for the tournament. Of his practice rounds he said, "I've been sort of fiddling around out there for awhile. Now I try to fight it a little. The course is hard, fast and will continue to get faster, particularly with the cut greens. I looked for a lot of irons off the tee. But I'm happy with the course and the conditions."

In his first Open in 1963 at Lytham, Jack seemed on the verge of winning before misplaying the 17th hole and finishing third. He was second to the late Tony Lema

at St. Andrews in 1964. Then, in 1965, he finished nine strokes behind Britain's Peter Thompson. He broke through in 1966, beating Doug Sanders with a birdie and par on the final two holes. The next three years he failed again, finishing second to Roberto De Vicenzo in 1967; second to Gary Player in 1968 and sixth to Tony Jacklin in 1969.

Nicklaus also seemed doomed to lose to Sanders in 1970 when the latter missed a four-foot putt and forced a playoff. Jack won—but not before he almost blew a four-stroke lead. In 1971, at Royal Birkdale, he finished sixth to Trevino. Indeed, this seemed to be the one tournament Nicklaus could not dominate. His game faltered and it didn't matter what course he played on.

In 1972, however, the British Open was once again being held at Muirfield and Nicklaus liked the course. The 5th, 11th, 17th and 18th holes were lengthened, which seemed more suited for Nicklaus' long game. The rough, once knee high, was cut, but it still remained a tough test of golf.

"The tougher Muirfield is, the better chance I'll have," Nicklaus said. His main competition would come from Trevino, defending the title he won the previous year, and upset with his game to this point of the season. It wouldn't be easy for Nicklaus.

The British Open ended the dream for Jack Nicklaus, for that year at least. He is still young enough and good enough to challenge for the Grand Slam for the next five to eight years. But it was more than his inability to win this tournament that did him in. It was Lee Trevino, "Supermex," the man who most likely will stand in the way of every major championship or future Slam Nicklaus seems to have in his hip pocket. No longer is it Arnold Palmer, Billy Casper, or Gary Player who challenge. They are still capable of winning tournaments and will be among the top money-winners every year for several more to come. But Trevino is the threat, and he proved it again at Muirfield.

In contrast to the fair-haired and quiet Nicklaus, Trevino is a dark-skinned, happy-go-lucky golfer who enjoys talking to galleries, joking with them and laughing at himself. To other golfers, his habits are annoying. But somehow Trevino manages to keep his concentration and wit at the same time. And after three days he held a six-stroke lead over Nicklaus.

Jack hadn't come this far, however, to lose without a fight. For three days he played a conservative game, hoping it would be enough to win. Now, on the final day, he reached back for everything he had and began making the kind of charge Arnold Palmer became famous for. Six strokes behind a golfer of Trevino's ability is insurmountable for just about everyone except Jack Nicklaus. On he came, birdie after birdie, and at one point, he actually held the lead.

The string of birdies ran out at

Colorful Doug Sanders lost the 1966 British Open to Nicklaus by a stroke.

the 12th hole and Jack parred that one as well as the 13th, 14th and 15th. He bogeyed 16 and missed a chance to birdie 17 when he hit a poor drive. Heading for the final hole, he trailed Trevino by one stroke.

The 18th hole is a famous par-four, 470 yards with a complete complement of bunkers, traps and unruly rough. The green is long and narrow and it was expected that Nicklaus would pull out his driver and make his final charge. He reverted to his conservative style of the previous days, however, and used a 1-iron. On his second shot, he hit a 5-iron and left himself 30 feet short of the cup for the birdie he would almost certainly need to tie Trevino and force a playoff. Those watching surely thought Nicklaus would stroke the putt hard and risk running by the hole rather than falling short. It was something Palmer would do. Instead, Jack played it safe again and his putt fell two feet short of the cup. He made his par but lost by one stroke. The strategy might have worked if it weren't for the tournament-saving shot Trevino made at the 17th when he sank a chip shot to save his par. Buoyed by his sensational shot, Lee boldly took out his driver at 18 and hit a shot that was expected of Nicklaus. His 7-iron left him on the green, only seven feet short of the pin. The British Open belonged to Trevino for the second straight year. Perhaps he wasn't the technician Nicklaus was, but it was his human behavior that made him boldly hit that chip shot and then use the driver on the 18th, while Nicklaus consulted his textbook and used an iron.

Americans had hoped to give Nicklaus a big welcome home in expectation of the fourth and final leg of the Grand Slam, the PGA. It would have been the sports story of the year, bigger perhaps than the World Series or Super Bowl. The galleries would have been overflowing and newspapermen, magazine writers and television crews would have almost doubled the population of Oakland Hills, Michigan, site of the PGA. It was a difficult course, fitting for the championship at stake. And while the PGA was still not a title to sneeze at, the glamour had been lost at Muirfield.

Nicklaus came into the tournament recovering from an infected finger and the disappointment of not winning the British Open. He was one of the favorites, but it seemed from the outset, the PGA might belong to someone else in 1972. The battle of Muirfield had even taken some of the fight out of Trevino, who was as jovial as ever but not as sharp with his game. The PGA would go to Gary Player this year, the black-clad little South African who still wins more than his share of money and titles, though he is only a part-time player on the tour.

Nicklaus started with rounds of 72 and 75 and seemed to have little interest in the proceedings. It disappointed many in the galleries who hoped he would make an effort to at least win three fourths of the Slam. On Saturday, the third day of the tourney, Jack regained the touch and shot a 31 on the front nine. He smiled again and seemed to enjoy playing golf. But the course does not give in to even a Nicklaus, and Jack finished with a 68. On the final day he shot a 72 and finished at 287, tied for 13th place. Meanwhile Player seemed assured of winning as his competition faded in the rough of the Oakland Hills course. For a time it appeared Player would follow them as he bogeyed two holes and drove into the rough on the 16th.

"I was really demoralized," Player said. "I'd worked hard; I always do for this major championship. I felt that it was mine to win and here I was this close—and it was slipping away."

Looking through the trees Gary could see the green 150 yards away. "I didn't want to hit a 9-iron 150 yards, but I had to get up over those trees," he said. "It was either going to be a three or in the lake."

It was a three. Player's shot landed three feet from the cup and he tapped in the putt to win. He finished with a final round of 72 to combine with earlier rounds of 71-71-67- for 281. It was good enough for a two-stroke victory over Jim Jamieson and Tommy Aaron. It was a big victory for the

Among the young stars starting to challenge Nicklaus is Lanny Wadkins.

popular Player and an interesting tournament. In other years it would have been received with more enthusiasm, but this was supposed to be the climax to Jack Nicklaus' quest for the Grand Slam and Jack wasn't the only one disappointed.

In the same manner Bobby Jones' father had trained him at an early age to handle a golf club, Nicklaus started his education early. His father was a pharmacist in Columbus, and spent hours telling his son about the accomplishments of Jones. Jack, like Bobby Jones, had an interest in other sports also, and played baseball, football and ran track while in school. He worked after class in his father's drug store and always assumed he would attend Ohio State. He met his wife, Barbara, during her freshman year and married when he was a senior.

Jack began playing golf at 10, when he followed his father around the Scioto Club course. The pro there was Jack Grout, who became Nicklaus' instructor. It was Grout who taught Jack to hit with as much power as he could on every shot.

"Just hit it out of trouble and don't worry about how you look," Grout said. Nicklaus was a fast learner and even as a 10-year-old was shooting a nine hole score of 51. By the time he reached his early teens, Jack was beating most of the local golfers at the club. It was more impressive since the Scioto course had been the site of several U.S. Open Championships.

"Even then, you could see he had a chance to be special," Grout said. "I never saw a kid hit a ball that far or that hard."

By 13 Nicklaus was breaking 80 and at 16, he won the Ohio Open, finishing ahead of several pros. But the improvement hadn't been all that steady.

"I remember the 51 I shot the first time out, but the second time I shot 61," he said. "Then, for weeks, I got worse and worse."

As an early teen, Nicklaus felt his oats and thought he was accomplishing a great deal. But his father was quick to point out that Bobby Jones was junior champion of his father's club at the age of nine, amateur champion of Georgia at 14, champion of the South at 15 and tied for fourth place in the U.S. Open by the age of 18.

"Whenever, I got too big for my britches, that usually did the trick," Nicklaus says.

Nicklaus did qualify for the U.S. Amateur championship seven times and won it in 1959 and 1961. He made his initial appearance in the tournament in 1955 when he was 15. It was then that he met Bobby Jones for the first time. The competition was being held at the Country Club of Virginia in Richmond, and Jones came specifically to see the youngster who was being compared to him so favorably. He watched from the gallery as Nicklaus hit drives with the strength of a full-grown man.

"On the 11th tee, I saw him in the crowd," Nicklaus recalls. "I started getting shaky all over. I was so excited I hooked my drive into the woods. Then I overpowered a chip shot and drove over the green on the 13th. I was

Billy Casper beams after one of his tour victories over Nicklaus.

so nervous I don't remember if I even held the clubs properly. Then I saw him head back to the clubhouse, and I felt terrible."

Jones was impressed with what he saw, however, and later wrote a letter urging Nicklaus not to turn pro. By the time he was 19, Jack was elected to the U.S. Walker Cup team and helped it to a 9-3 victory over Britain at Muirfield by winning both his matches. In 1959 he lost only one of his 30 matches. Two years later he won the Amateur again, and decided to turn pro.

"I know I disappointed a lot of people, but I didn't know what to do. Everything happened so fast I was confused. I was still trying to earn my degree from Ohio State. I had an insurance business I was trying to get off the ground. I decided to devote all my time to golf." It was a move that disappointed Jones, but it would have been unfair to criticize Nicklaus. There was a lot more money in golf and the purses were going to get bigger. Jack could always retire or return to insurance if he grew tired of golf. But the insurance business wasn't going to make him rich and his ability with a set of golf clubs could. It was a decision he would never regret.

"I just hate to play that big happy kid," Arnold Palmer said at the time. And so did a lot of other pros on the tour.

Nicklaus had lost to Palmer by two strokes in the 1960 U.S. Open, when he was still an amateur. "If I was playing that well, I thought I might as well get paid for it," he said. "I wasn't born a rich kid. Money like they were offering on the tour seemed like all the money in the world."

His first tournament as a pro was the U.S. Open in 1962 at the Oakmount Country Club in Oakmount, Pa. It was held in mid-June and Palmer was at the height of his career. Jack seemed unimpressed. "I want to be the best golfer the world has ever seen," he said.

He drew Palmer as a playing partner the first two rounds and that meant being subjected to "Arnie's Army." The exuberant and devoted followers of Palmer have little regard for the golfers playing with their hero. Nicklaus, even then, seemed unconcerned. He ignored Palmer and the galleries as he set his sights on the Oakmount course.

"I had been at Oakmount since Monday and I had played some practice rounds," he recalls. "It's a big sucker of a course and I decided I could control it. I decided to hit everything as hard as I could, because it was easier for me to go over the trouble spots than to go around them."

After the first round, Nicklaus had a 72. Palmer was at 71 and Gene Littler led with a 69. Nicklaus shot a second-round 70, but Palmer had a 68 and a share of the halfway lead with a total of 139. Jack was three shots back. The final round was to be a 36-hole marathon, the normal procedure for the Open before television made it a four-day tournament. Stamina as well as ability would be tested. After the morning round Nicklaus had gained a stroke on Palmer with his 72. The confrontation was inevitable and the afternoon promised to be interesting. Nicklaus played his slow, steady game while Palmer stayed in front. Then, on the ninth hole, Arnie made his first mistake when he had a bogey-six on the par-five hole. Nicklaus settled for a par and now was just one stroke back. It remained that way until the 13th, when again the veteran Palmer bogeyed and Jack had a par. Now they were even and stayed that way through the finish. An 18-hole playoff was needed and the next day, Sunday, it was held with a national

Who can ever forget Lee Trevino's stirring 1972 British Open win.

audience watching on television.

Nicklaus shot a 71 to win by three strokes and the end of Palmer's dynasty was in sight. "Nobody figured me to win anyway," Nicklaus said. "I figured I had no reason to play scared or cautious. They all thought Palmer would win; I had nothing to lose."

Jack had become the youngest Open winner in the history of golf. He took the measure of the best golfers on the tour and then beat the best of them all in a head-to-head match. "It was kind of satisfying," Nicklaus says.

He did it with his power, the ability to drive a golf ball 300 yards on occasion and in the 275-yard range most other times. He accomplished this while claiming his game is based on just two fundamentals.

The first is a simple one—to keep the head completely still throughout the swing. It is taught to weekend and future pro golfers alike, yet some never master it. Nicklaus claimed it took him two years to learn not to shift his head when he swung. Sometimes Grout would have an assistant hold on to Nicklaus by his yellow locks to keep his head in place.

The second lesson Grout taught his prodigy was to roll the ankles inward to maintain balance. On the backswing, the left ankle rolls in toward the right and the right ankle returns the favor on the downswing. "If you go over beyond your right instep on the backswing, if you relax the pressure there, you are dead," Nicklaus says. He claims to have spent four or five years mastering these two basic and, on the the surface, simple fundamentals.

The results made it worthwhile. After winning more than $60,000 on his first year of the tour, Nicklaus reached $100,000 in 1963 as he won the Masters, PGA, Tournament of Champions, Palm Springs Classic and Sahara Invitational. For his opponents on the tour, the worst was yet to come. In 1964, his earnings climbed to $113,284 to lead the money-winning list. His biggest triumph was in the Tournament of Champions. In 1965 he took down prizes worth $140,752 and won five tournaments, including the Masters. He won the Masters again in 1966, though he got "only" $111,419. In 1967, he won the U.S. Open in what he has often described as "my best tournament considering everything."

The success continued, even during the years in the mid-to late 1960s when his critics said Nicklaus had lost interest in golf, that he was now a businessman first and did not have enough drive to win. Purses had risen to an extent that a pro did not have to win or even place second or third in any tournament all year to earn over $100,000. At one time, just a decade ago, only one or two pros would win $100,000. In 1972, there were several over $200,000. Observers, for instance, have said Arnold Palmer has reached the end of the line, that he can no longer be considered one of the favorites in a major tournament. Yet, "poor" Arnie had still won over $100,000.

And as a result of the purses, Nicklaus could be seen on television doing commercials for airlines as well as endorsements for golf equipment. He is more personable than in his first years on the tour, though he still retains the image of a slow, meticulous and bland man on the course.

"Competitive spirit is something inside a man," Nicklaus maintains. "People are different and their make-ups are different, and this is mine. I don't think I could change if I tried, and I don't care to try. It has worked for me. Sure, I get as nervous before and during a tournament as anyone. But I guess it just doesn't show on me. That doesn't mean I'm loafing or lackadaisical. It's just the way I am. I think I want to win tournaments—the big ones and the rest too—as much as the next guy."

Nicklaus speaks in that squeaky voice which seems to rise even higher when he is defending himself from his detractors. "I just can't help it if I don't show my feelings on the outside. If I don't set my jaw and jangle my change and tug at my hat, it doesn't mean I don't care. It doesn't mean I don't have the desire. It's just my way. Golf is my life, and I am not going to have anybody tell me how to run it or how to behave. There is no proper way. I just do it my way."

Despite his failure to win the Grand Slam in 1972, Nicklaus will undoubtedly make other attempts. It's more than merely entering the four major tournaments. The psychological preparation is just as great. And with the financial security that is now his, there is no need for Jack to enter so many tournaments every year. He can pick and choose, keeping his game competitively sharp while preparing for the Masters, U.S. Open, British Open and PGA. He has gotten rich in golf, but no one should feel that Jack Nicklaus loves the game any less than Bobby Jones, who retired an amateur at the peak of his career.

"To Jones golf was a sport of integrity, not dollars," says Jack. "Unfortunately for golf, I'm afraid too many pros on the tour play the game for commercial value only. Maybe it's easy for me to say, now that I've made a nice living from golf. But if I ever lose sight of the fact that golf is a sport, then I will lose sight of the meaning of the game. If I were paid a salary to play golf, then I'd give the game up."

It would have been impractical for Nicklaus to have remained an amateur, unless he was independently wealthy by birth. He confessed talking to Jones about it several times.

"Believe me, I had many thoughts about trying to follow in Jones' footsteps and staying an amateur. But as he (Jones) agreed, economically, in my time, you cannot do that. I also feel an amateur can't reach his potential today because his competition is so limited."

Jack Nicklaus has reached his potential and he should remain on top for years to come. How does he rate with Jones, Sam Snead, Ben Hogan, Arnold Palmer and the golf greats from the earlier years? Is there anyone now emerging on the scene who can be as dominant as Jack has been for the past 10 years? Perhaps the judgment cannot be made until several years after the stocky blond has called it quits. He wonders about it himself.

"I talked about these thirteen major championships for so many years. Now I have them, and I'm so dumbfounded I don't know what to say. I look at myself and ask 'Am I that good. Do I deserve to be there?' "

Jack Nicklaus is that good and few will ever be there with him. ■

Once shy and withdrawn, Nicklaus now responds warmly to his galleries.

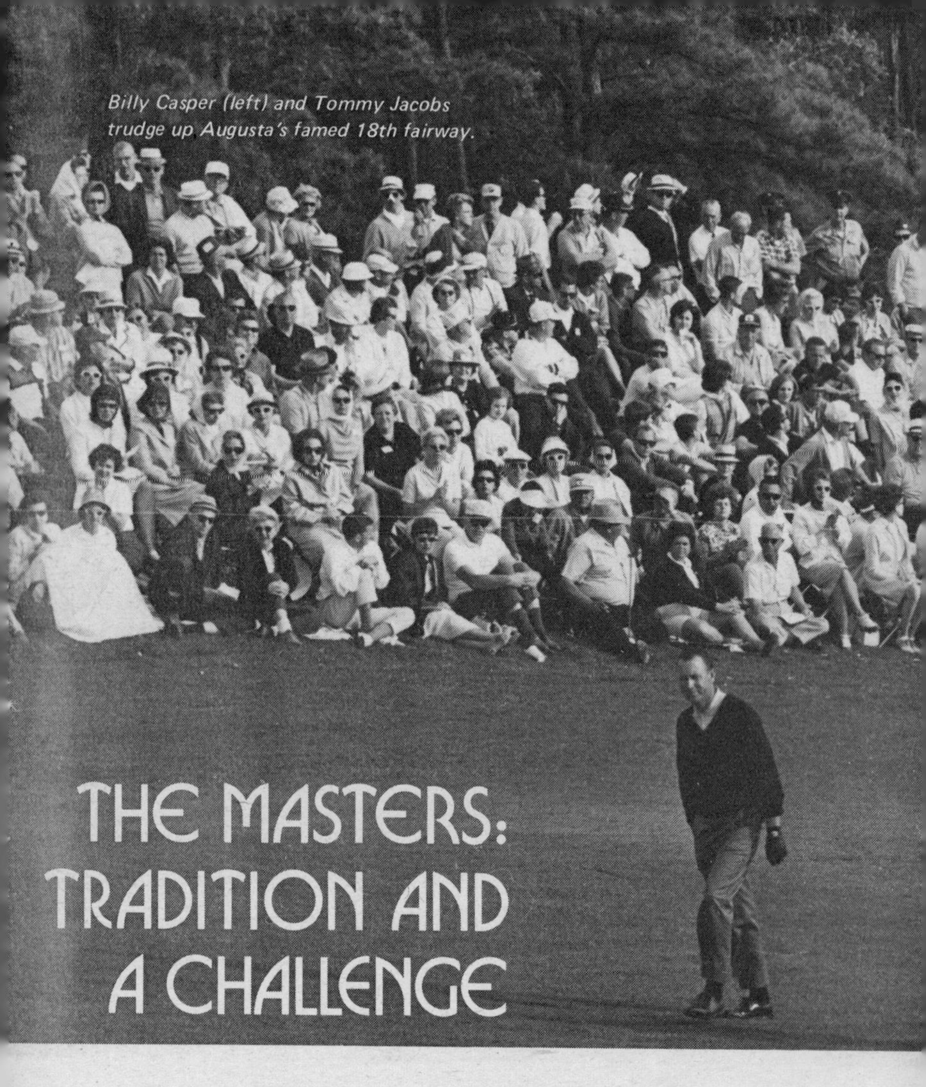

Billy Casper (left) and Tommy Jacobs trudge up Augusta's famed 18th fairway.

THE MASTERS: TRADITION AND A CHALLENGE

■ Spring comes early to the South, while the Midwest and East are still suffering through the lingering winter months. Golf enthusiasts quickly sweep snow off the front porch and then watch sun-tanned players tee off on television. It's in the spring that the Masters is played.

Winter is kind to the South, where a snowstorm is merely a light dusting or flurry. The land begins to turn green again in March, though the melting frost leaves it soggy and soft. By April, college students are sunbathing on campus lawns and some begin to plan a weekend in Augusta. They're not alone. The golf season may last around the calendar, but

it seems to really begin with the Masters when all of the sport's big names meet for the first time of the year.

Sometimes the weather doesn't cooperate with the magnitude of the event and blustery winds and rain make the Augusta Country Club course more difficult to play. Sometimes the galleries stay huddled together to keep warm and the golfers sport varied and colorful sweaters. They'd gladly trade those sweaters in, though, for the green coat that goes to the champion.

The Masters Tournament is part of modern golf's Grand Slam and the credit for it goes to the only man to win the Grand Slam,

Bobby Jones. It was Jones who laid the groundwork for the Masters after winning the Slam in 1930. At the time he probably never dreamed the Masters would become one of the four most coveted championships in golf. Purses weren't high in Jones' day and he played the game purely for love. He started and finished his career as an amateur and returned to his home in Atlanta, Ga., to devote his time to fulfilling the dream of building the ultimate golf course.

It would be the perfect course, one that embodied all the challenges of the world's finest courses. It would be built on scenic land with natural beauty that would not be altered. It would be a course that could challenge even Bobby Jones, a player who seemed able to take any course apart when he put his mind to it. Jones found the land he was looking for in Augusta at an old plantation called Fruitlands. And he found the backing he would need from Cliff Roberts, a successful New York banker. Together they began a search for friends who were willing to contribute. The dream was becoming reality.

Jones wanted only a privileged few to play the course and so he formed a private club with members selected on a national basis. Only 30 would be chosen but membership fees were surprisingly low at $350 and annual dues were $60.00.

But the course Jones had built was too attractive to escape the attention of the U.S. Golf Association, which asked him to make Augusta the site of the 1933 Open championship. However, the members had viewed their club as a status symbol and weren't about to share it with the rest of the touring pros. They rejected the U.S.G.A.'s request.

As it turned out, the members were not opposed as much to the idea of using the course for a national tournament as much as they were against having outsiders running it. Why not start a tournament of their own? The idea was well received and in 1934, just one year after they had turned down the U.S. Open, the Masters was born.

Jones objected to the name at first, deciding the tournament did not deserve its title. Perhaps he felt the course wasn't challenging enough. For whatever reasons, the name was changed to the Augusta National Invitation.

So, in 1934, 72 golfers teed off in the Augusta National-Masters tournament. In reality it was the Bobby Jones Open, the product of four years' work. And though he objected at first, Jones was persuaded by Cliff Roberts to enter the competition himself. He joined the likes of Horton Smith, Paul Runyan and Craig Wood, the best of their day. Roberts felt Jones would give the tournament the publicity boost it needed, one that would make it a fixture on the pro tour.

If the tournament had been played in Hollywood, no doubt the screen writers would have had Jones returning to competitive golf with a flourish and conquering both his fellow golfers and the course he himself helped conceive.

Four-time Masters winner Arnold Palmer chips out of Augusta rough.

But the four years away from competitive golf had taken the edge away from Jones and he shot a 76-74-72-72–294, 8 strokes behind the winner, Horton Smith, who shot rounds of 70-72-70-70–282. The tournament was a success, however, and members of the Augusta National club decided to make it a yearly venture. In 1935 they also changed the name back to the Masters.

Whether the tournament would have grown to become as popular had it remained the Augusta National is questionable. But as the Masters it quickly became famous all over the world. Some tournaments offer more in prize winnings–some even double those of the Masters–and some carry more exposure from television, notably the 1972 U.S. Open at Pebble Beach. There are several tournaments that bring more endorsements. And one big-name golfer, Lee Trevino, refused to play at Augusta for several years, claiming the course was not suited for his game. Yet, when one thinks of American golf, he thinks of the Masters.

The Masters is steeped in tradition and has an advantage over the other tournaments that comprise the Grand Slam because it is held at the same site every year. For some, it's a horror show every time out. They know the course; they can play it blindfolded. And still their scores never improve except for an occasional good round. Then there are others like Arnold Palmer and Jack Nicklaus, who have won the tournament four times each.

Even when one begins to dominate the Masters, the club refuses any alterations of the course or its format. The Masters is synonomous with tradition and the television cameras do not turn off their red lights until the winner has donned the green blazer. No one receives a check for his victory until after that moment, and perhaps it is because of Jones' influence. He put tradition and the game before money and the green coat symbolizes that. Many have performed the ritual, from Byron Nelson to Jack Nicklaus, Arnold Palmer, Gary Player, Ben Hogan, Craig Wood, Sam Snead, Gene Sarazen and Billy Casper.

As the years go by, the names become more famous and the shots more memorable. There was Sarazen's double eagle on the final round of the 1935 Masters, a 220-foot shot that enabled him to tie Craig Wood and eventually win by five strokes in the 18-hole playoff. The only other double eagle was recorded by Bruce Devlin, a quiet Australian who achieved the distinction in 1967.

Each hole has its own personality, each has its own nickname to the golfers. Some are spoken of in awe, others in fits of frustration. There's White Pine, the first hole; Carolina Cherry, the ninth; and the 15th hole, Fire Thorn. The course totals 6,980 yards when it plays at maximum, and the best round was recorded in 1940 when Loyd Mangrum shot a 64. It was equaled in 1965 by Nicklaus.

The course was actually designed by Dr. Alister MacKenzie, with the help of Jones. It was a difficult course but fair, and one with few bunkers and other unnecessary hazzards. As first designed, the course played the reverse of today. The first through ninth holes formed the back nine in 1934. But in 1935, the nines were switched as an experiment. It remained that way and, through the years, improvement was concentrated on the finishing holes. Five of the back nine became water holes compared to no water holes on the front nine.

Water, distance and television cameras glamorized the back nine and they were the setting for Arnold Palmer's famous charges and other memorable finishes. Even the nicknames seemed more exciting, Rae's Creek—the 13th hole—and Amen Corner, for the 15th, a par-5. The front nine were forgotten to all but the golfers, many of whom thought the opening holes were tougher than the back nine.

The first hole is par-4 and 400 yards, with the tee situated just below the clubhouse veranda and the practice putting green just off to the side. The drive must carry over a valley and land on a plateau that is bordered by a bunker on the right. From there it takes a pitch shot to reach the green. It's a hole that gives a golfer the opportunity to get off to a good start.

If there is to be a hole-in-one at Augusta, the chances are it might be made on the fourth hole, a par-3, 220-yarder. Golfers like

Big Jack Nicklaus is another who has won The Masters on four occasions.

Nicklaus and Palmer take dead aim at the wide expanse of green and ignore the risk of finding the bunker in front of it. For Nicklaus, a player who averages 275 yards with a driver, an iron is sufficient on the fourth hole.

"If you can get past the fifth hole under par, you have a right to expect a low score," Palmer once said. Easier said than done for most pro golfers. The fifth is par-4 and 450 yards. It's a hole among the pines and requires a blind approach shot to the green. The green falls away, and a shot hit too forcefully will keep rolling to a lower level that requires a steep putt coming back up to the hole.

While the sixth through the ninth also remain mystery holes to the American public, the golfers greet them with a sigh of relief.

The sixth hole is another birdie hole. It's par-3 and 190 yards where the green lies below an elevated tee. In earlier Masters, there was a huge mound to the right of the green. It has been reduced in size in recent years.

The seventh hole requires more finesse than power. It is a 365-yard, par-4 with a raised green that is surrounded by four bunkers. It is a hole that looks as if it would produce many birdies, but the pitch shot to the green requires such delicacy that many golfers often play it safe and settle for a four. Those who try for the birdie often land in one of the bunkers.

The eighth hole is 530 yards and a par-5 that is uphill all the way. The ninth was once the finishing hole, but now it merely signifies the turn for the TV cameras. It is a 420-yard, par-4 challenge, where the tee shot heads down a hill and the pitch shot heads back up—another blind approach to the green. The green is fast and slopes downward, much like the 18th hole. Many putts have never stopped rolling until they were well past the cup.

But as beautiful and dangerous as the front nine holes are, they

South Africa's Gary Player was first foreign player to win Masters.

are merely the window dressing for the finish. They make Augusta one of the great challenges in the game. This is why an invitation to the Masters is the goal of every young golfer. The club does not issue them freely and in recent years has come under fire from various factions which question its exclusive policies. There are some who say it discriminates against the black golfer and there are those who believe Trevino, a Mexican-American, snubbed the tournament because of these policies rather than his objection to the course.

The image of the Masters has withstood the attacks, however, and is not tarnished in the least. It is still the tournament American golfers want to win the most.

"It's not so much the money," Nicklaus says. "You know you really have done something important in golf if you win the Masters. Heck, even just playing in this one is enough."

If the man who is recognized as the best golfer in the world feels that way about the Masters, then he probably speaks for most of his counterparts. And it also speaks well of Bobby Jones who turned an old plantation into part of the Grand Slam.

When people mention the great Masters of the past, they inevitably start with Gene Sarazen's "impossible" shot in 1935. It occurred during the fourth round when Craig Wood apparently had the championship won. He finished with 282 and was in the clubhouse waiting to try on the green coat. Sarazen was still on the course, but he needed three birdies on the final four holes to tie Wood.

Gene started his comeback on the 15th, the par-5, 520-yard hole that is called Fire Thorn. It was a straightaway with several bunkers and a pond. All he could do was wind up and hit as far as he could.

"My drive had been a good one, exceptionally long," Sarazen says. "I was paired with (Walter) Hagen and as we walked up the course following our tee shots, we heard a roar. Wood had carded a birdie on the last hole, and was in with a 282. When we reached our lies, I asked my caddy, 'Stovepipe, what do I need to win?' 'Boss,' he said, 'you need four threes.' Well, I figured I might as well go for broke; I was bound to lose anyway."

Sarazen chose a four-wood and walked up to the ball that was lying 220 yards from the pin. "I hit it hard," Gene recalls. He then watched it travel no more than 20 feet off the ground toward the hole.

"I was behind a small hill, and couldn't really follow the ball," he said. "I watched it until it disappeared, and then I heard a roar. I suspected then that the ball had gone in, but I really couldn't believe it. Sometimes, I still can't. But I made the double-eagle two."

Still slightly shaken by that shot, he parred the 16th and 17th and was still a stroke behind Wood. But on the 18th he earned a tie when he knocked in a three-foot birdie putt to set up an 18-hole playoff the next day. By this time Wood was completely unnerved. The green coat he thought was almost his was now

being sought by Sarazen. After 26 holes the next day, the Masters was finally decided. Sarazen shot 36-35-36-47–144, while Wood came in five strokes behind.

Sarazen's charge has helped make many leaders sit nervously in the clubhouse over the ensuing years. But Jack Burke Jr. probably never thought he'd be able to match that comeback when he began the final round of the 1956 Masters eight strokes behind the leader, amateur Ken Venturi. Venturi led after three rounds with a total of 210. The galleries were just a bit more excited than usual, aware of Ken's chance to become the first amateur to win the tournament. Privately, Bobby Jones was probably rooting for him, too. Burke was just one of the also-rans, not even close enough to challenge for the lead that final day. But Burke did more than challenge—he won!

Byron Nelson, a Masters winner, was also coach for Ken Venturi.

Venturi's coach had been Byron Nelson, a former Masters winner who gained an automatic invitation to all future Masters. He was usually paired with the leader on the final round, but his relationship with Venturi was so close, that Bobby Jones decided to break up the team. Instead of Nelson's steadying influence, the 24-year-old Venturi was paired with Sammy Snead, who himself was still in the running.

Venturi was not a master on that final round, as he shot an 80. Burke wasn't having a great round either, merely one like his previous three of 72-75-71. In fact all he did was shoot another 71 and it was good enough to win with a total of 289. Despite the blow-up, Venturi was next at 290 and Cary Middlecoff was third with a 291. Snead finished fourth at 292, tied with Lloyd Mangrum.

The 289 total is still the highest ever recorded to win the tournament, though it had been reached first in 1954 when Snead and Ben Hogan tied. Hardly anyone noticed Burke's score, however, because of the drama involved. After 16 holes, he was still behind, but birdied the 17th while Venturi took a five and Middlecoff a double-bogey six.

Until 1961, no one but an American pro had ever won the Masters. Venturi came the closest of any amateur and no foreigner had made a bid. That ended in 1961, when a small, quiet South African named Gary Player conquered the Augusta course. He had turned pro in the United States in 1957 and did not exactly burst to the top of the money-

Billy Casper took 1970 Masters title after playoff round.

winning lists. He won $3,286 in his first year and rose as high as $18,591 in the next three years. In 1961, at 25, Gary reached the top of his game. He won $60,540 and, more important, he won the Masters.

Though small in stature, Player is strong and always fit. He used to be easy to pick out on the course in his black shirt and slacks and white hat—although today he varies his dress more. He had won two earlier tournaments and was co-favorite with Arnold Palmer. Palmer took a stroke lead over Player on the first round, shooting a 68. The second day, they reversed their scores and were even at the halfway mark. But on the third day it appeared Player would win easily when he shot a 69 to take a four-stroke advantage over Palmer, who soared to a 73.

However, even Player was aware of Palmer's magic. He knew how "Arnie's Army" could lift him to the top of his game. He knew how Arnie could come charging back from any deficit. And there were always those earlier Masters to think about, how Sarazen and Burke accomplished the impossible. No one thought the word "impossible" applied to Arnold Palmer.

And true to his style, Arnie came rushing back on the final day. He made up the four strokes and, heading for the 18th, he held a one-stroke lead. But this time the Masters was one hole too many for Palmer. With Player as his partner, Arnie drove into a bunker to the right of the 18th green. Another amateur, Charlie Cole, had made a bid and was closing in. An amateur, a foreigner

Huge galleries jam Augusta each year when Masters tradition is renewed.

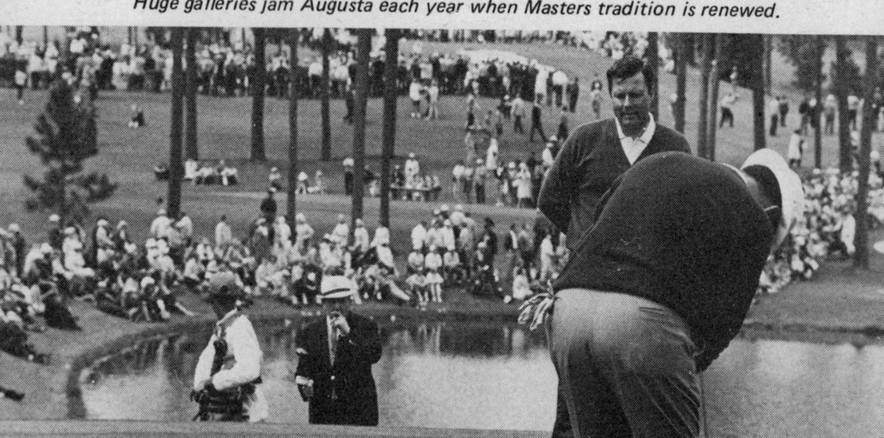

and an American pro. The odds leaned heavily to Palmer.

Arnie misplayed the 18th, though, taking a six getting out of the bunker and into the cup. He even missed a short putt that could have tied him for the championship and forced a playoff. Player came home in four and the unflappable South African had won. Cole closed fast to tie Palmer for second.

For Gary Player the 1961 Masters was the turning point of his career. He has gone on to win every leg of the Grand Slam at one time or another. Most recently he won the U.S. Open for a second time in 1972—wearing his black shirt and slacks with matching white hat.

The tears that Palmer wiped away on the 18th hole at Augusta in 1961 turned to a big, infectious smile the following year. He won the Masters for the third time, but only after an 18-hole playoff, as the tournament produced its first triple tie. It included Palmer, Player and Dow Finsterwald, a surprise.

Palmer didn't make it easily, however. After shooting rounds of 70, 66 and 69 in what seemed like a personal vendetta against the course for the previous year, he ballooned to a 75 on the final day. It left the three men tied at 280. Finsterwald had started the final round two strokes behind Palmer, and Player was four back. Putting problems plagued Arnie as he stumbled around the course he knew so well. Finsterwald shot a remarkable 65 on the third round to get into contention, but he too was unsteady on the last day. Player made up four strokes; he could have won, but he missed the opportunity.

Palmer wasn't going to suffer through the humiliation of the previous year. He shot a 68 in the playoff while the best Player could do was 72. Finsterwald dropped out of sight with a 77. Only Jimmy Demaret and Snead had won the Masters as many as three times and now Arnold Palmer had joined them.

Four years later, in 1966, the second three-way playoff was needed when Jack Nicklaus, Tommy Jacobs and Gay Brewer tied for first. Seventeen players had led or shared the lead during the four rounds and no one could pull away. The three had tied with a total of 288. In the playoff Nicklaus played the steadiest and finished with a 70. Jacobs battled him but fell two strokes back at 72. Brewer skied to a 78. With that victory Nicklaus also became a three-time Masters champion. He was in good company.

The most controversial Masters was played in 1968. Perhaps an indication that it would not be the same perfectly-run tournament as it had been in the past came when Ben Hogan pulled out because of a bad knee and Bobby Jones attended at the last minute, though his health was failing. Jones did not go out on the course and did not participate in the winner's ceremony.

Roberto De Vicenzo shot a 65 on the final round, but history will record it as a 66. And it cost the man from Argentina a possible Masters green coat. He started the final round at 212, two strokes behind Gary Player, the leader. Tommy Aaron was third at 213. De Vicenzo quickly captured the galleries when he sank an eagle two on the first hole and immediately tied for the lead. He went on to shoot an incredible 31 on the front nine to go five under for the round. For 30 years Roberto had toured the world to play golf, his travels taking him from Nairobi to Augusta. A likeable, congenial man, he is easy to root for and had won 140 tournaments. His only major championship, however, was the British Open. And now on the final Sunday at Augusta, he had a shot to win the Masters on his 45th birthday.

The 31 on the front nine gave De Vicenzo a one-stroke lead over Bruce Devlin. Bob Goalby was third, two strokes back. Roberto did not try to protect his lead on the turn for home. The final nine holes must be played aggressively and one stroke is not a safe lead. He parred the 10th and 11th, then birdied the 12th to go six under par. He couldn't shake Goalby who was still coming on. A birdie at eight and pars on nine and 10 left Goalby within range, two strokes back.

Both men continued to answer the other's challenge. A birdie by De Vicenzo was greeted by a roar from the crowd. Moments later, another roar went up from several hundred yards away. Goalby had given his answer. After the 17th hole, De Vicenzo was tied at 12 under with Goalby who was on the 15th. The 17th hole would be a memorable one for De Vicenzo.

Both players wavered a bit on the final holes but when Goalby sank a short putt on the 18th, the scoreboard showed two red 11s, signifying they had tied for the championship. A playoff would be needed the next day. Goalby had a final 65 and so did De Vicenzo. Or so they thought.

In the press tent, it was discovered that Aaron, De Vicenzo's playing partner, had marked Roberto's card incorrectly at the 17th hole. He wrote a 4—a par for that hole—while De Vicenzo had actually scored a birdie three. Roberto had signed the scorecard and, according to Rule 38, Paragraph 3 of the Rules of Golf, "a score higher than actually played must stand as returned."

That changed De Vicenzo's score to 66, a stroke higher than Goalby. There would be no need for a playoff; Goalby was the winner of the Masters. Roberto was gracious and blamed himself. Goalby, an old friend of De Vicenzo, said he would rather have won in a playoff.

When Bobby Jones was informed of the error, he made it clear he wanted to know if there were any ways to waive the rule. There weren't and finally he asked if there were any other loopholes. Informed there weren't, he sighed, "that's all I want to know."

Jones was grief stricken that day. After 35 years his tournament had suffered its first blemish. But Bobby wasn't about to place himself above the rules of golf. The decision stood and Goalby was the winner. It was a tarnished victory, but it was the Masters and many golfers would gladly take it—any way they could. ■

U.S. OPEN BELONGS TO EVERYONE... EXCEPT SAM SNEAD

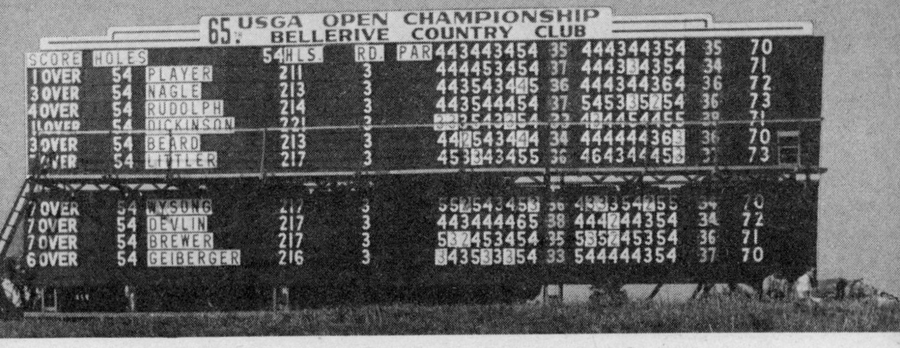

Scoreboard for the 65th U.S. Open at Bellerive CC in St. Louis.

■ To trace the beginning of the United States Open would be to trace the origins of golf back to Scotland and the British Open. Though other tournaments are more glamorous and some provide more prize winnings, the Open is to American golf what the World Series is to baseball and the Super Bowl to football. It's not merely a tournament, it is a display of nationalism.

This is why the tournament does not have one permanent site. To borrow from Woody Guthrie's song, "This Land is Your Land," the Open belongs to everyone, from Inwood, N.Y. on the East Coast to Pebble Beach on the shores of the Pacific. It's been played on courses that some golfers have termed "cow pastures" and it's been played in every part of the country, some where it will be remembered as the greatest event to ever occur in that particular community.

For many years the U.S. Open also set itself apart from other tournaments because the final round was 36 holes. The Open would begin with 18 holes on Thursday and 18 more on Friday just like most tournaments. But come Saturday, the test would begin—one of strength, stamina and golfing ability. It was on Saturday that even the critics of golf could not argue that it took a true athlete to play the sport. Those who watched football, baseball, basketball and hockey had often questioned golf's masculinity. How could anyone call it a sport when 50 year-old men could compete with athletes in their teens? What physical exertion was needed after hitting the ball, except walking after it? How could a man five-foot-five compete with one who was over six feet?

Some of the questions remained unanswered after the Open. But they were eventually answered when the football and baseball players picked up golf clubs and experienced for themselves the mental and physical exertion the game demanded. More than one threw down the clubs in frustration. And though some could hit a ball 300 yards, few had the finesse to pitch a shot to the green, avoiding bunkers, and then stand motionless over a putt, steady of hand and mind.

And the U.S. Open did qualify as one of the more grueling sports events of the year because of those final 36 holes on Saturday. Most of the time they were played under a hot summer sun and no golfer could feel ashamed to call it quits before the end of the tournament. This is what set the Open apart; this is what made it the true golfing test.

The men who run the United States Golf Association are practical, though, and when television came calling, they broke with tradition. They said it was too tortuous to continue playing 36 holes of golf on Saturday. What they meant was that the TV money was too attractive to turn down. Television extended the Open to Sunday when the final 18 holes were played in front of a large national audience. No one would succumb to the heat now. The challenge of the 36 hole wind-up was gone. The Open became another four-day extravaganza but the golfers did not seem to mind.

As was mentioned before, however, the origin of the Open came long before radio, much less television. It was in 1888 when a group of traveling New York golfers decided they'd like to build a course in the United States that was equal to one they had visited in Scotland. They realized this dream when the course was built on a Yonkers, N.Y. farm. It was the country's first course, although it was a modest three-hole layout.

By 1894 golf had begun to catch on in the U.S. and in December of that year, nine men formed the United States Golf Association. They represented five of the most important golf clubs in the country: the St. Andrews Club in Yonkers, which borrowed the name of the famous course in Scotland; the Newport Golf Club in Newport, R.I.; the Country Club in Brookline, Mass.; the Chicago Golf Club in Wheaton,

U.S. Open has been one frustration after another for great Sam Snead.

Ill., and Shinnecock Hills in Southampton, L.I.

John Reid, who laid out and played the original St. Andrews club in Yonkers, was chosen as the first president. And in order to promote their new organization they decided on an official tournament that would be "open" to all. It was an official tournament and was called the Open. The Newport club was awarded the first tournament and it was played on Oct. 4, 1895.

It is interesting to contrast the origin of the Open with that of the Masters, a tournament that extended invitations to only a few. And while the process was originally meant only to insure the best field possible—a hand-picked choice of golfing's best—it eventually led to charges of racism in the mid 1960s. There would be no such charges against the Open.

The first tournament was only 36 holes and Horace Rawlins of England was the winner, turning in rounds of 91 and 82 for a 173. By today's standards, he wouldn't even have made the cut. But it has to be remembered that in 1895 the clubs were wooden and the balls did not travel with the distance and accuracy they do today. Under those conditions, Rawlins had a good round.

The equipment and scores remained the same through the early 1900s or until the advent of the Roaring Twenties when technology provided better clubs and a higher velocity ball. Rawlins, though, had left his mark. It was the first Open and he became both the first foreigner and youngest player ever to win it. He was 19 years old at the time, an age when American golfers nowadays are taking their scholarships and going off to college to try and win an NCAA championship.

Though the tournament was open to all, the people attending the first Opens were comprised of socialites and leaders of business and industry. They were the only ones who could afford memberships.

To this day golf has remained something of an aristocratic sport, still associated more with men of wealth than laborers and the poor. For one thing many can't afford

Jack Nicklaus won Open titles in 1962, 1967 and 1972.

even present day membership fees for private clubs. Those who aren't private club members awake at dawn on their days off and head for the long lines at the public courses.

In the ghettos and lower middle-class neighborhoods, kids grow up dribbling a basketball on the hard city concrete or playing baseball with splintered bats in an empty lot strewn with broken bottles. Golf is a rich man's game to them—a symbol of success in life.

It's changed to a certain degree; many of today's youngsters are able to learn the sport if they so desire. The costs aren't as great as they once were and people are better able to afford them. It's led to the great influx of young talent, "the rabbits," as they're called by the established pros and news media.

In 1895 the U.S. Open was truly a social event and Newport won the right to be the host because the America's Cup yacht races were being held there. It was originally planned for September but pushed back to October to avoid conflict with the Cup festivities.

After the first Open, acceptance was slow in coming. The tournament became part of the National Amateur. After the three days of Amateur competition, the Open would begin. The Amateur was the big tournament of the time and the USGA hoped the crowds would stay to see the Open and perhaps help hypo interest. It wasn't until 1898 that the Open severed its ties with the Amateur and went out on its own. It became a 72-hole tournament.

Under the new format, the first Open was played at the Myopia Hunt Club course in Hamilton, Mass. It was won by Fred Herd, a Scotsman. No matter how many times they changed it or started over, it seemed a foreigner would always win the "first" Open.

Herd did not distinguish himself on the course, but no one else did, either. He shot a four-day total of 328, an average of 82. But it wasn't the highest winning score in the Open. That came three years later when Willie Anderson spent 72 holes searching through the rough, and won with a total of 331. Anderson took four Opens, which ranks him with Bobby Jones and Ben Hogan as the men who have won the most. Anderson won three in a row, 1903, 1904 and 1905.

The Open has been interrupted only twice and both times by the reality of World War. In 1917 and 1918 it was canceled because of World War I, and World War II brought a halt to the Opens of 1942, 1943, 1944 and 1945.

Nothing else has been able to put a dent in the most important tournament in the country and perhaps the world. A depression and other smaller wars such as Korea and Vietnam have failed to cancel it. Golfers like Sam Snead, who now compete in Senior tournaments and only one or two others, make a point of playing in the Open. It has been an especially frustrating tournament for Snead, who has never won it. He's finished second four times.

While the Open is held at a different site every year, only the toughest courses are selected.

HOLE
18 MOODY
18 BEMAN
18 ROSBURG

They include Baltusrol in Springfield, N.J.; Oakmont in Oakmont, Pa.; Oakland Hills in Birmingham, Mich.; Merion Cricket Club in Haverford, Pa.; Congressional in Washington, D.C.; Winged Foot in Mamaroneck, N.Y.; Bellerive in St. Louis, and Inverness Club of Toledo, Ohio.

Golfers don't turn down the Open for any reason. Some, like Snead, keep hoping for the miracle that would earn them their first Open championship. It's a tournament filled with memorable victories and also marked by the men who should have won and didn't. There was Bobby Jones and his victory in 1930 on the way to the first and only Grand Slam. There was Ben Hogan, coming back from a near-fatal automobile accident to win the Open in 1950. There was Ken Venturi, battling the heat and a physical handicap that would end his career, to win the 1964 Open.

There's Jack Nicklaus with three Open titles. The first tournament he won after turning pro was the Open. How Snead must have envied him! Arnold Palmer will be a favorite in the Masters even as he grows old because of his success there. But in the Open Palmer has managed to win just one (1960) while finishing second four times.

For the foreign players who once dominated this tournament, victories are now rare. Only Gary Player and Tony Jacklin have been able to take the title away from an American in recent years.

Player became the first foreigner to win since Ted Ray in 1920, when he won at Bellerive in 1965. He did it in a playoff against Australian Ken Nagle. Both had shot 282 in the four regulation rounds and then Player fired a 71 in the playoff while Nagle bowed to the pressure of the Open and finished with a 74. It was the first "Television" Open, as the tournament was spread over four days for the first time. Another first, another foreign champion.

Jacklin won his Open in 1970 at the much ridiculed Hazeltine National Golf Club in Chaska, Minn. While American golfers sent a never-ending stream of complaints to the tournament officials because of the course, Jacklin, a 25-year-old Englishman, played it with the usual British reserve. He was the only golfer to finish the tournament under par, with rounds of 71-70-70-70-281. He won by seven strokes over Dave Hill, one of the most vocal critics, who came in with 288.

Some of the golfers' complaints were legitimate. Winds of over 40 miles a hour blew on the first round, making it especially difficult to play. Jacklin handled it, though, and some said it was because wind is a part of almost every tournament in Britain.

Jacklin increased his lead after every round. After encountering difficulty on the final day, he sank a 30-foot birdie putt on the ninth hole and was never headed. He was given a hero's welcome in England, and a few days later the crumpled winner's check was

Scoreboard tells story of Orville Moody's first-round lead in '69 Open.

found in a pair of trousers he was sending out to be dry-cleaned.

Two men owned golf in 1971 as Lee Trevino and Jack Nicklaus continued their spectacular duel for dollars and titles in the Open at Merion Golf Club in Ardmore, Pa. Both men had tied with 280 after 72 holes and a playoff was needed. The next day Trevino fired a 68 while Nicklaus had a 71. Nicklaus had missed an opportunity to win in the regulation 72 holes when his 14-foot birdie putt on the last hole was short. For Trevino, it was one of three Open titles he won. The others were the Canadian and British Opens. For the sixth time in nine years, the defending champion failed to make the cut.

Rarely does the Open serve to boost an unknown player to stardom. It's not a place for the inexperienced or the weak of grip. But how does anyone explain the 1969 Open won by Orville Moody, a 35-year-old Army veteran from Yukon, Ohio? Moody spent 14 years in the Army before joining the PGA tour in 1967. He remained anonymous and 1969 was only his second full year on the tour.

The Open that year was played at the Champions Golf Club of Houston. Moody beat Deane Beaman, Al Geiberger and Bob Rosburg, all by one stroke. Ironically, it was a year when none of the glamour names of golf was in serious contention. Moody finished the tournament with 71-70-68-72—281. He had played in the Open only once before and that was in 1962. He was still in the Army and failed to make the 36-hole cut.

Moody seemed unaware of the pressure. On the final day, eight players were within two strokes of one another and all of them were playing the final nine holes. Moody was the steadiest, even though he went over par on the 14th. He parred the last four holes to win.

Orville enjoyed the benefits from his victory as he appeared in television commercials, endorsing several products. But it also signified the highlight of his career. He has failed to win any major tournaments since. He also does not finish high on the money-winning lists.

Little did Arnold Palmer know in 1960 that the Open he won at the Cherry Hills Country Club near Denver, Colo., would be the only one he would manage to capture thus far. He did it in typical Palmer style, charging from behind on the final 18 holes.

Mike Souchak was the leader after three rounds with a 54-hole total of 208. But Palmer attacked the front nine, shooting a 30 as he birdied six of the first seven holes. He finished with a round of 65 to go along with earlier rounds of 72-71-72. His total was 280—two strokes better than runnerup, Jack Nicklaus, then only an amateur.

As pleasing as the victory was to Palmer, he does not have fond memories of the Open. His most disappointing moment in golf came in the 1966 Open at the Lake Course of the Olympic

Arnold Palmer won 1960 Open with 72-hole total of 280.

Ben Hogan's four U.S. Open titles added to drama of this great tourney.

Country Club of San Francisco. It seems Palmer is at his best when he is forced to come from behind, when the golfers ahead hear the cry of "charge" and the thunderous roar of the "Army" as Arnie makes his late bid for victory.

But Palmer seems out of place in the lead. With nine holes to go in the 1966 Open, Arnie led Billy Casper by seven strokes. Even a typical Palmer comeback by Casper would probably fall short. Arnie had gone out in 32 on the final round and needed par on the last six holes to break the record for lowest score. It was set in 1948 when Ben Hogan shot a total of 276. Palmer was within range of shooting a 274. Then, suddenly, he was in danger of losing the tournament altogether.

Casper gained a stroke at the 10th hole, another at the 13th, two at the 15th and two more at the 16th. He evened the match at the 17th and a playoff was scheduled for the next day. Palmer had soared to 278 and was a beaten man.

Casper won the 18-hole playoff, shooting a 69 while Palmer had a 73. Nicklaus was third and Gary Player, the defending champion, finished in a tie for 15th place. But the talk was of Palmer's collapse. Few golfers could lose a seven-stroke lead in nine holes and it seemed absurd to think a golfer of Palmer's prominence could do it. His army was stunned, having watched Casper make a charge their man had built his entire career on. The Open would never again be an easy tournament for Palmer.

There is a photo of Ken Venturi, taken after he won perhaps the greatest Open of them all. The photo was shot after he parred the final hole to win the 1964 Open at the Congressional Country Club in Washington, D.C. It shows Venturi looking straight up at the sky, a smile on his face and tears in his eyes.

"My God, I've won the Open," Venturi said.

His victory was more than just a man winning a golf tournament, even if it was the Open. It was a man overcoming great physical odds and a man who had lapsed into a three-year slump. His victory in the Open was called "a work of fiction."

The tournament belonged to three men at the start: Venturi,

Tommy Jacobs and Palmer. The first round belonged to Arnie, who shot a 68. The greens were baked hard by the heat and the course was one of the longest in the country. The greens were grainy, the golfers complained and the heat shortened tempers.

Palmer had his 68 for a two-stroke lead, however, and seemed relaxed and confident. Jacobs, then 29, was a bold player, a free swinger who figured to do well on the longer courses. He shot a 72. But the next day, he proved to be hotter than the weather. Jacobs toured the course in 64 strokes to take the halfway lead with a 136. Palmer shot a 69 and was one stroke back at 137. Where was Venturi? He was back in the pack with a 142.

Saturday would provide the ultimate test. If the sun had been unbearable on Thursday and Friday, it seemed twice as hot as golfers prepared to play the traditional 36 holes. The greens had been softened somewhat by a night-long rain, and Palmer, perhaps eager to take advantage of them before they dried out, went

Billy Casper smiles broadly after stirring win in 1959 U.S. Open.

for the pin aggressively with every shot. He missed the first five greens, hit the sixth, but then three-putted to fall four shots behind Jacobs.

At this point, Venturi unexpectedly entered the picture. He birdied the eighth hole at the same time Palmer was having difficulty on the sixth. It gave Ken his fourth birdie of the morning and as he walked up the fairway on the ninth hole, with his familiar white cap keeping the sun from baking his head, Venturi had passed Palmer and was in contention.

At the ninth hole Ken continued his dramatic round with another birdie. He took only 30 shots on the front nine and, believe it or not, Venturi was leading the Open. Even Jacobs had fallen victim to the Congressional course, bogeying the eighth and ninth holes.

All eyes were on Venturi. He was a golfer who burst on the national scene and rapidly rose to fame. Just as quickly, however, he faded from view. As an amateur he made the Walker Cup team in 1953. In 1956 he came close to winning the Masters as an amateur before shooting that fateful 80. Still, he lost by only a stroke. He lost two other Masters by slim margins and seemed to lose something in his game. Once a leading money winner, Venturi earned only $4,000 in 1963.

Ken failed to qualify for the Opens of 1961, 1962 and 1963 as he suffered a succession of physical ailments, ranging from back injuries to walking pneumonia. Then circulation problems caused him to lose the feeling in his hands. He was apparently through as a pro golfer.

Now came the comeback at the Congressional, though Jacobs quickly regained the lead on the back nine to shoot a 70 for a 54-hole score of 206. Venturi had a 68 for a 208, and remained in contention. The hope faded, however, when it was revealed that Ken had played the final five holes on the brink of near exhaustion. He drank some tea, took salt tablets and rested for 50 minutes. When he walked to the first tee for the final 18 holes, he was accompanied by a doctor.

Palmer jumped back into the picture in the afternoon after slumping to a 75 in the morning, six shots back. Jacobs double-bogeyed the first hole and Venturi was back in a tie for first. He appeared drawn and pale and walked like a man years older. But he kept making his shots and he was hitting the ball with authority.

He took the lead on the ninth hole as he sank a nine-foot putt for a birdie four. It then became clear that he was in contention to stay. He began to droop; his legs wobbled as if they were made of rubber. He moved on, from hole to hole, with the doctor by his side. Finally he reached the 18th, a par-4. He could still shoot a seven and win. The question was whether he could summon enough strength to finish the hole.

Venturi's tee shot was weak but accurate, and his second shot caught a bunker, 40 yards from the pin. He could still play it safe, but stroked a brilliant wedge shot

Ken Venturi is hugged by wife after dramatic 1964 U.S. Open triumph.

to within 10 feet of the cup. He made the putt and won the U.S. Open. The applause was deafening, but actually it had started earlier, when he approached the bunker after his second shot. The crowd greeted him then, and he shakily removed his white cap and waved it. The sun wasn't going to stop him.

In the air-conditioned clubhouse after the match, Venturi regained much of his strength and also his wit. In an age of nicknames for a golfer's following, Venturi thought he'd give a name to those who cheered him throughout the exhausting final 36 holes.

It wasn't Arnie's Army, but to Venturi they were worth just as much. "For years all I've ever had was Venturi's Vultures," he said.

The very next year the tournament was lengthened to four days. The scene of Venturi struggling down the fairways would not be repeated. But in a sense, it was Venturi, in his anguish, who displayed the championship form and courage the U.S.G.A. had strived for when the Open format was decided upon. If it had been any other tournament, Venturi may never have gone back out to the first tee that Saturday afternoon. But this was the Open and no one passes up such a challenge. ■

THE P.G.A. TOURNEY:

■ Once a year they gather together in a selected part of the country for an old-fashioned lodge meeting. They're all there, the shop stewards, the ordinary members and the executive branch. The Professional Golfers Association meeting is called to order. "And after lunch, let's all go out and play 18 holes."

The PGA tournament is better known as one of the legs of golf's Grand Slam. But it is also symbolic to the men who participate in the tournament because the PGA is their own event. It's a raffle and a union meeting all in one. Most of the proceeds from the event go to the PGA. To golf, it is what the all-star game is to baseball and the Pro Bowl is to football.

The formation of the Professional Golfers Association came about in 1916. It was set up like many of the labor unions at the time—to protect a small group of men participating in the same business. Touring pros were not highly looked upon then; no one asked them to endorse shaving cream on radio or in the local newspaper. The pro golfer was looked upon as a second-class citizen and was barred from country clubs and major tournaments, which catered to amateurs whose families were wealthy. It is where golf originally got its image as the sport of the affluent. Only those who could afford the country club surroundings might be expected to compete for the amateur titles and first-place belts that were awarded.

But enough men had found the ability to wield a set of clubs, and enough had found the lure of travel too great to resist, to prevent the growth of the sport on a pro level. Compared to office work and regular routines, the touring pro's day seemed glamorous and challenging. People seemed to overlook the fact that, even then, not everybody made

BY THE PROS... AND FOR THE PROS

Gary Player accepts trophy after winning first PGA title in 1962.

the cut and golfers found it hard to earn a living chasing a small round ball.

In 1916, they joined together and the PGA was formed. It consisted of teaching professionals and touring pros. They joined as one to form an organization that would work for them. It would strive to improve their lot, and attempt to upgrade the events and increase the amount of prize money that was being offered. Hopefully, the PGA would make the profession of golf a respectable one—even to the people behind the walls of the country clubs who thought that, on the outside, the sport was in the hands of barbarians. Rodman Wanamaker, the Philadelphia store magnate, had a great influence on the PGA. He played a vital part in the formation of the organization and came up with the idea of a golf tournament which would belong to the members—"The Championship of the Professional Golfers Association of America."

The late, great Walter Hagen won five PGA titles in his prime.

It was an idea that met with overwhelming approval, for it provided the pros with an identity and some added prestige for their infant organization. The first PGA tournament was held between October 10 and 14 at the Siwanoy Country Club in Bronxville, New York. Sectional qualifying rounds produced 32 entries, and the first victory went to James Barnes, who had to outlast the best players of his day in Jock Hutchinson, Willie MacFarland, Tom Kerrigan and Walter Hagen.

Dow Finsterwald won the first PGA tourney at stroke play (1958).

Barnes' victory was his first of two straight, although they came three years apart—the PGA tournament had to be suspended for 1917 and 1918 because of World War I. When the war ended and the tournament resumed, Barnes showed he hadn't lost his touch. The man nicknamed "Long Jim" won again in 1919.

While the U.S. Open and Masters have always been stroke play tournaments, the PGA started as match play competition. Match play was considered to be the only true test at one time as it matched one man against another. Strokes did not matter—the player who won the most holes was the victor. It was the gentleman's way of playing golf and there were many wealthy amateurs who belittled the pros' stroke play.

The amateurs were convinced that to win a hole was the only way to keep score. A score of 1-up means the golfer won by one hole. A golfer who won 7 and 6 had a seven hole lead with six holes to play. But, while the PGA kept to tradition and played by match rules, the country had changed and was clamoring for stroke play.

So strong were the PGA's ties to the past, that it did not abandon its match play format until 1958. It wasn't totally the doings of the pros, either. In fact they remained split on how the tournament should be conducted. But the public seemed unanimous in its lack of interest in the event. So it was the public—and television—more than the pros who led to the adoption of stroke play in the annual PGA tournament. Dow Finsterwald was the first winner of the revamped PGA as he fired a four-round total of 276 to beat Billy Casper. The tournament was held at the Llanerch Country Club in Havertown, Pa. It helped set the game back on a course that would eventually make it one of the more popular sporting events in the country.

However, through the years no man did more to help the image of the PGA than Walter Hagen. Some considered Hagen the best shotmaker in the history of golf. Those who followed Ben Hogan might argue that point, as would the fans of Jack Nicklaus. But no one who watched Hagen would disagree that he was one of the most colorful golfers ever to play the sport. He was flamboyant, fun-loving and carefree. He was so loose on the course that it served to psychologically unnerve his opponents, who were shaken by Walter's blithe spirit.

Hagen was a man who spent money freely, who didn't care to save any of it. He was one who truly believed "You can't take it with you."

"We only come this way once," he said, "and we should smell all the flowers along the way."

Once, when asked to play in the 1920 British Open, Walter arrived only to find the Deal Club was off limits to the second-class pros. They—and it included Hagen among them—were told to dress in a pro shop far from the course. Needless to say, the combative Hagen would not have any part of those rules. "Not me," he said. "The Haig" ordered a long limousine, parked it at the front gate of the country club and changed in the car. He also hired a

chauffeur who doubled as a valet-footman. The chauffeur met him at the 18th hole each day with a drink and a clean polo shirt.

In 1926, when the PGA was still match play, Hagen put his gamesmanship to work to win the event held at the Salisbury Country Club in Westbury, Long Island. His opponent was Leo Diegel.

From the beginning, Hagen began conceding putts of four and five feet. Diegel was flabbergasted because Walter was not the kind of golfer who would give anything to an opponent. He accepted these "gifts," but gradually began to suspect that "The Haig" was up to something. Late in the match Diegel chipped up to within two feet of the cup. He figured Hagen would concede again, especially since he had been giving putts of twice that length all day. But Hagen just stared at the sky when Diegel looked at him.

"There must be a roll here I don't know about," Diegel said to his caddy. Suddenly, he was shook up over a two-foot putt. He hesitated, wavered, looked back at Hagen and finally putted. He missed—naturally—and Hagen went on to win the PGA championship 5 and 3.

Because of his antics, Hagen carried the PGA with him. Walter brought glamour to the event, because the public was attracted to him. He still holds the record for most PGA victories with five—in 1921, 1924, 1925, 1926 and 1927. His four consecutive PGA titles are also a record. In addition he reached the final round six times and won 22 consecutive match play victories in the tournament.

Unlike the Masters, which is held in Agusta, Ga., every spring, the PGA is switched to a different site with each renewal. In 1972 it was held in Oakland Hills, Mich., and in previous years it has been held at places like the Firestone Country Club in Akron, Ohio; the Aronomink Golf Club in Newtown Square, Pa.; the Oakmont C.C. in Pa.; the Scioto C.C. in Columbus, Ohio; the Miami Valley C.C. in Dayton, Ohio; and the Seaview C.C. in Atlantic City, N.J.

All the greats of golf have won the PGA—including Hagen, Tommy Armour, Hogan, Sam Snead, Byron Nelson, Chick Harbert, Jack Nicklaus, Gary Player, Julius Boros and Bob Rosburg. One of the ironies is that Arnold Palmer has never won this coveted leg on the Grand Slam.

It is a tournament that has had its share of drama—and yet it may have missed out on becoming the greatest golf event of all time in 1972, when Nicklaus failed to win the British Open after taking the first two legs of the Grand Slam, the Masters and the U.S. Open. Oakland Hills, a quiet suburb of Detroit, was preparing for the invasion of reporters, television crews and fans from all over the world. Preparations were taken long in advance and clocks were stationed in the press room with times of cities all over the globe. If

Gary Player (with gray-haired Joe DiMaggio) won second PGA title in 1972.

Nicklaus had won the British Open, the PGA would have been the most publicized golf event ever. Instead, Jack lost to Lee Trevino and Oakland Hills lost its chance for golf history.

Ordinarily, the 1972 event would have been hailed as one of the most exciting PGA tournaments. But the letdown from Nicklaus' defeat couldn't be compensated for. Gary Player won his second title and did it with a miraculous shot on the 16th hole of the final round. For Player, it helped quiet the talk that he, like Arnie Palmer, had reached the end of the line as far as winning major tournaments was concerned.

"I've always said golfers were the worst lot of athletes in sports," Player maintains. "All others train for their game, but most of us just go out and play. I try to stay in shape, though, and I think this is why I won the PGA. I was stronger at the finish—when it counted."

Gary made his remarkable shot on the 16th hole when he took out a 9-iron and shot blindly over the trees toward the pin, 150 yards away. The shot landed four feet from the hole and Player called it "the best shot I've ever hit. If I don't hit it perfectly, I'm in the water," he said.

When Player reached Detroit, he was asked by a young reporter whether he thought he could ever win another "big one." He was also asked if he thought he was still a member of the Big Three

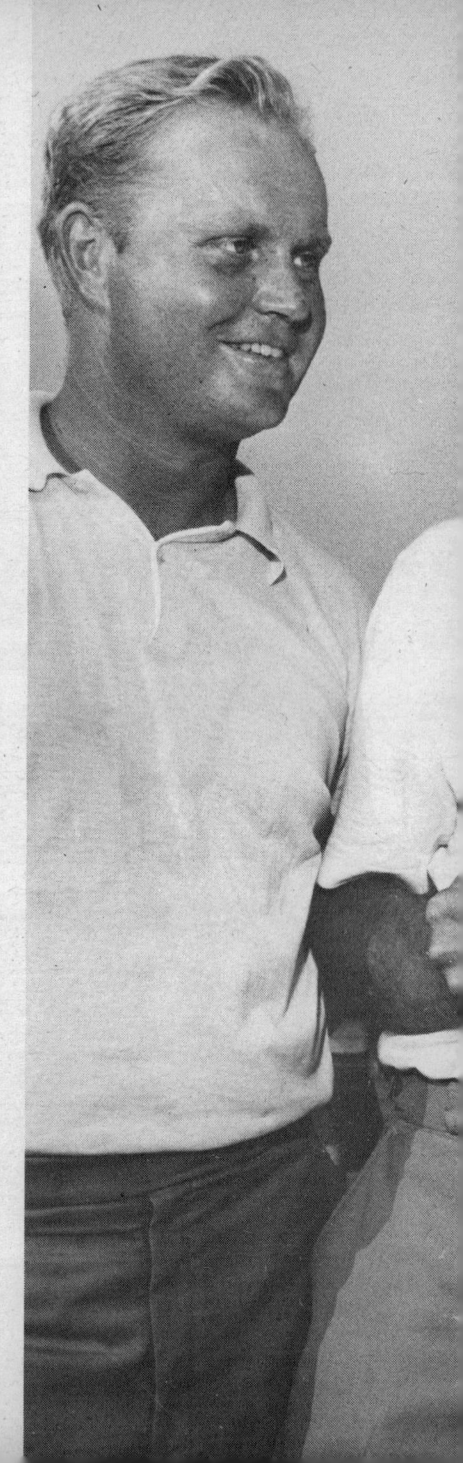

Dave Marr (center) with Nicklaus (left) and Casper after '65 win.

ANNUAL
CHAMPIONSHIP
PROFESSIONAL
GOLFERS
ASSOCIATION
AMERICA

which included Nicklaus and Palmer. Player said he thought he could win another major tournament but never considered himself part of any Big Three. The reporter translated that into an over-the-hill confession by the South African.

"I'm just reaching my peak," says Player, now 36. "I'm as fit as anyone in the world my age, have won more titles (36) than anyone in the modern era and more money than anyone other than Jack Nicklaus. That story was unfair."

Player took it out on the course and was given extra incentive when he received a phone call of encouragement from his father, early Sunday morning, before the final round began. "Without getting too dramatic," Gary said, "my father had an overdraft at the bank when he wrote a check to send me on my first overseas golf trip. And that gamble has paid off. When I talked to him on the phone you could hear it in his voice, what this means to him. He was all choked up. And he said, 'just win that tournament for me.'

"You know what this means because you all have fathers," Gary adds. "He worked in the gold mines for 31 years and never made more than $500 a month. I spend that much on phone calls each week when I'm away."

Player went on to win one for his father—and he did it in dramatic form. It was one of the best-run PGA tournaments in the history of the event. Yet, in some ways, most of the potential drama had been lost when Nicklaus' bid for the Grand Slam failed. If Jack had won the British Open, the PGA would have been more than a golf event. It would have been golf history.

Long-hitting Bobby Nichols took the 1964 PGA title with 271 total.

One of the more memorable PGA events in the early days took place in 1938 when Sam Snead, winner of three titles, took a beating. It's the PGA he remembers more than the ones he won. Snead was already a well-known and accomplished golfer in 1938. He had won several tournaments, had finished high up in many others and was playing at the top

Arnold Palmer has won everything in sight—except the PGA championship.

Little Jerry Barber took 1961 PGA title in a special playoff.

of his game during the early rounds of the PGA.

When Sam reached the final round, after several one-sided victories, he was considered a prohibitive favorite. And when it was determined that his opponent would be the weak-hitting little Paul Runyan, Sam was considered a shoo-in. An automatic victory, some said.

It was—but for Runyan. Paul had a precision-like short game which helped make up for his lack of hitting the ball a long way. Runyan shot a 67 in the morning round for a five-hole advantage over Snead. The crowds at the Shawnee Country Club in Delaware, Pa., were stunned, but figured Slammin' Sam would come back in the afternoon. He had done it before. Runyan still hadn't made believers of the galleries.

But they all underestimated Runyan. The little guy increased his lead to seven holes after nine holes in the afternoon. He kept applying the pressure and defeated Snead, 8 and 7. To this day it remains the biggest margin of victory in any PGA match.

Snead finished as runner-up again in 1940 when Byron Nelson beat him by one stroke at the Hershey C.C. in Pennsylvania. Finally, Snead prevailed in 1942, beating Jim Turnesa, 2 and 1. He won again in 1949 and 1951—the latter victory over Walter Burkemo, 7 and 6, which made up for the embarrassing defeat he had suffered 13 years earlier when everyone conceded Snead the victory except little Paul Runyan.

As has been mentioned, by

Bob Rosburg (left), with PGA official, was surprise winner in 1958.

Al Geiberger is interviewed by press after stirring 1966 PGA triumph.

1958, the public had grown tired of the match play format. Even the players took sides, with most on the side of the stroke play approach. Finally, the PGA announced its historic decision and the great stars of the 1950s lined up to take a shot at winning the first "modern" PGA. Snead was entered, as well as Ben Hogan, Billy Casper, Arnold Palmer, Jay Hebert, Tommy Bolt, Gene Littler, Doug Ford and Player. However, it was the lesser-known Dow Finsterwald who walked away with the title.

A native of Ohio, Finsterwald had always been accused of playing conservatively. He never took chances, never gambled on hitting over water and never cut the corner of a dogleg. As a result, he rarely came up with sub-par scores. Finsterwald seldom shot a 67 but then, he rarely shot a 75, either. That was until 1958.

With a field of big hitters to contend with, Finsterwald opened with a 67, three under par, and it was a total he could not have achieved without taking several chances. He came in with a more acceptable (for him) 72 the second day, tying him with Jay Hebert for the halfway lead. Dow shot a 70 in the third round, but Snead had begun a charge that took him to the lead with a three-round total of 207. Casper was a stroke back and then came Finsterwald. Entering the final day, Dow knew his normal style of play would not be good enough to catch Snead. He had to gamble;

he had to take a reckless shot now and then.

Finsterwald's play that day would make Arnie's Army blush with envy. He went out in 31 on the front nine and then turned for home, still blazing hot. He finished with another 67 and won by two strokes over Casper with a total of 276. Snead was third at 280. Finsterwald had changed his style to win the biggest tournament of his career.

Another relative unknown was Bobby Nichols, who had been a pro for four years without achieving much distinction. He always showed the potential, finishing high among the leaders in most tournaments, but seldom finishing on top. By 1964, Bobby had won three tournaments but the PGA was not expected to be his fourth, especially since the event was being held at the Columbus Country Club in Ohio, the home course of Jack Nicklaus. Even then, Jack was considered the big favorite.

Nicklaus had won the PGA championship in 1963 and was trying to become the first man to win it back-to-back in stroke play. But Jack's bid ended the first day when Nichols shot an incredible 64. His ball hit trees and bounced into the middle of the fairway. His iron shots held the greens and his putts were seemingly magnetized by the cup. He had eight birdies and 10 pars and dropped in birdie putts of 30, 20, 15 and 10 feet.

Nichols was in front and stayed there every round to the finish. After three rounds he had a 204 and his 72-hole score of 271 was the best ever in the tournament. The promise that Nichols displayed in the earlier years finally blossomed in Nicklaus' own backyard.

No one has really dominated the PGA tournament since the legendary days of Walter Hagen and the era of Snead. Even Nicklaus has been unable to dominate, winning the championship just twice—in 1963 and 1971. Other winners in recent years include Dave Marr in 1965, Al Geiberger in 1966, Don January in 1967, Julius Boros in 1968, Ray Floyd in 1969 and Dave Stockton in 1970.

In the public's eye the PGA probably ranks behind the U.S. Open, Masters and British Open in glamour and importance. But to the golfers themselves it is "their" tournament, the one they administer, sponsor and operate without outside financing to provide the prize money and the expenses.

The pros are grateful for the success of golf, naturally, and are thankful for the interest shown by television which has helped increase the purses. But they are proudest of the PGA, the tournament that has become symbolic of the struggles the pro had had in the early days when he was treated with as much respect as a pool hustler.

So it will be a rare day when a big name in golf misses the PGA tournament. Even Nicklaus, despondent over his loss in the British Open in 1972, played at Oakland Hills. After all, what would the meeting of lodge brothers be without him? ■

THE BRITISH OPEN: PRESTIGE NOT PURSE

■ Every year the best American golfers join others in their trade from different parts of the globe and make a pilgrimage to Britain—to the rugged coasts of Scotland where the wind whips briskly off the Atlantic and carves legendary golf courses out of the terrain. They are known as St. Andrews, Hoylake, Lytham, St. Annes, Troon, Carnoustie, Birkdale and Muirfield—and they are synonymous with the tradition of the British Open.

When the golfers come to one of these ancient courses (or links) it is not to praise it, but to play it. While the winner of the British Open does not reap a monetary fortune by U.S. tour standards, the prestige and subsequent rewards are enough to make the British Open one of the most coveted golf championships in the world. And to the people of Britain and the rest of Europe, no American, despite the reputation he may have built for himself in the States, has achieved true

In 1969, Tony Jacklin was the first Englishman to win the British Open in 18 years.

golfing greatness or earned their respect until he wins the British Open.

This is why they all make the journey across the Atlantic, to the birthplace of golf. And while Americans have been known to complain about conditions of courses in the U.S., not a murmur is heard when they begin driving the smaller British golf ball through the turbulent winds and cold drizzle that mark the weather in that part of the world. In 1860 they played for a challenge belt; today it's for money. But what they are really competing for is a place in golf history. That's why the British Open is part of the golf's Grand Slam.

The British Open began in 1860, but the idea for such a tournament had circulated for several years prior to that. When the Open finally became reality, it was through the efforts of a small band of golfers who played at the Prestwick course. In 1851 they gathered at the Red Lion Hotel and founded the Prestwick Golf Club, electing the Earl of Eglinton as captain. They established an entrance fee of one pound and tacked on another pound every year to maintain a golfer's status in the club. In 1853, they persuaded Tom Morris, one of the early big names in golf, to leave St. Andrews and become club pro at Prestwick. They paid him a salary of 15 shillings a week. It was just three years later that these men—considered professionals and thus held in low esteem as opposed to amateurs at that time—decided to institute a golf tournament for Scotland. The idea for the British Open was born.

A committee was appointed and it included R. Whyte-Lelville, O.G. Campbell, Robert Hay and J.O. Fairlie. Their proposal was well received by most of the Scottish clubs and even those in London expressed an interest. Although at first the Prestwick club members had intended all clubs to have a share in running the tournament, the complications were such that they decided to take all the responsibilities upon themselves.

They listed several proposals in 1857, among them that the tournament was to be run at St. Andrews, that only two golfers from each club would be allowed to participate, and that a committee of four be formed to manage the event. Of the proposals only the last remained intact when the first British Open was finally held three years later. In the summer of 1860 invitations were sent to seven professionals working in Scotland and to one exiled Scot, George Brown of Blackheath. The tournament was played at Prestwick.

The field included Tom Morris, Robert Andrew, William Park, Alexander Smith, William Steel, Charles Hunter, George Daniel Brown and Andrew Strath. It was a 36-hole stroke play tournament and the winner would be awarded the challenge belt made of red morocco mounted with plates of silver containing the names of players and clubs. The terms of the competition were that the belt must be gained by the same player for three straight years before he

The British Open is one of Arnie Palmer's many titles.

would be entitled to keep it.

The Prestwick course consisted of only 12 holes, so the golfers played three rounds. Park and Morris emerged as the first men to dominate the championship with Morris winning four times and Park three in the first eight years. They were the two greatest golfers of their time and the rivalry helped build interest in the tournament.

Also helping to draw both crowds and golfers to the event was the decision made by the Prestwick committee prior to the 1861 tournament. They declared the event "open to all the world" and the field immediately doubled. Morris won again. In 1863 the committee announced there would also be money prizes in addition to the challenge belt, whereupon Park gained a measure of revenge by beating Morris. Gradually, the championship took on more meaning and by the 1870s, the Royal and Ancient Golf Club as well as the club at Edinburgh had joined with Prestwick to provide a winner's cup and rotate the tournament each year.

More so than Prestwick, the Royal and Ancient Golf Club gained prominence as the most famous site of the British Open. Once every three years the tournament was to be conducted at St. Andrews. It was held at the end of the club's autumn meeting, in late September or early October. Tom

Kidd was the first Open winner at St. Andrews, taking the belt in 1873. Although a native of that city, he was virtually unknown and was considered little more than a caddy.

The British Open has such a long and storied history that its past can be broken down into eras, and several of the tournaments can be categorized as milestones. Such was one in 1890 when the title left Scottish hands for the first time—and was won by an amateur, no less. John Ball of Hoylake was the man to win both distinctions. The late Bobby Jones was the only American amateur to ever win the British Open.

What surprised people most about Ball's victory was not the fact he was an amateur. Instead, it was because he was English and the proud Scots were reluctant to admit anyone else could be as good at the game as they were. In 1876 at the age of 15, Ball had participated in the Open at St. Andrews and finished sixth, eight strokes behind the winner, Bob Martin, and ahead of 28 other players. He won the British Amateur an amazing seven times and had won it again in 1890. Four months later he completed the sweep by winning the Open at Prestwick.

Lee Trevino won back-to-back British Opens in 1971 and 1972.

Ball had grown up learning to play the wind and nature's other hazards, so he prospered in the stiff northwest wind that blew on the day of the championship in 1890. He had a first round of 82 and then was the model of consistency as he came in with a second 82 on the final day to win by three strokes. He took home the Cup, but no money.

In the years immediately following Ball's victory, sentiment grew for an expansion of the tournament from 36 to 72 holes. The entry lists were growing every year, with 82 contestants seeking fame by 1891. Finally, in 1892, another milestone was reached when the championship was expanded to 72 holes. It was played at Muirfield and another amateur, Harold Hilton, emerged as the winner. The evolution of the British Open was complete.

The list of British Open winners reads like a Hall of Fame of golf. Harry Vardon, who won it six times; Ted Ray, Walter Hagen, Tommy Armour, Jim Barnes, Bobby Jones, Henry Cotton, a three-time winner; Ben Hogan, Peter Thompson, Kel Nagle, who won the 100th Open in 1960, and

Jack Nicklaus is another two-time British Open winner.

Gary Player, always a British Open threat.

finally the big names of recent years, Arnold Palmer, Gary Player, Jack Nicklaus, Lee Trevino and Tony Jacklin.

Perhaps Jacklin's victory will be remembered as one of the most popular of modern times. A native of England, Tony was a hometown favorite who ended foreign domination of the British Open after 18 years. Jacklin's victory was greeted with the same appreciation that Britons gave Henry Cotton, who ended a 10-year domination of the event by Americans with his victory in 1934.

Cotton had instituted a series of rookie of the year awards in the seasons following his retirement and one of the winners was Jacklin. Cotton saw promise in the youngster, which Jacklin started fulfilling in 1966 when he won tournaments in Africa and New Zealand. He played for England in the Canada Cup matches in 1966 and won his first big British event the following year when he captured the Pringle Tournament, and also won the New Zealand P.G.A. championship. Tony won his first American tournament in 1968 in the Greater Jacksonville Open which established him as a golfer of world-wide repute. He had been a pro for only six years.

The 1969 Open was held at Royal Lytham and Jacklin opened with a 68. It put him two strokes behind Bob Charles, the first round leader. Charles shot a 69 the next day to hold the lead while Jacklin fashioned a 70. Christy O'Connor, a veteran Irish golfer, shot a round of 65 to move into contention with Americans Orville Moody and Billy Casper close behind. Not to be overlooked was Peter Thompson, a five-time winner who was within striking range.

But even the finest of golfers have difficulty in an event such as the Open. Rarely can anyone put four good rounds together and, as play started that third day, some observers wondered when Charles was going to have his "bad" round. They didn't have to wait long as he slipped to a 75.

The championship was up for grabs—just the right atmosphere for a young golfer who might otherwise feel the pressure if he were engaged in a two or three-man battle with established players. Jacklin played another steady round and moved in front with his 70 for a total of 208. Charles was 210 along with O'Connor, who stumbled to a third round of 74. At 211 was Thompson and perhaps two bigger threats—Roberto De Vincenzo and Jack Nicklaus. The Bear was making his move.

The final round began with Jacklin and Charles paired. Charles cracked first, and then Jacklin thrilled his fans with a birdie on the third hole and another on the fourth hole, when he sank a 13-footer. He was setting a hot pace which cooled momentarily at the fifth when he recorded a bogey. But the young Englishman recovered at the seventh when he made a brilliant shot from the sand to score another birdie.

With nine holes to play, Jacklin had opened a four-stroke lead over De Vicenzo. Then came Charles, O'Connor and Thompson five strokes back. Then, one-by-one, they all began fading from sight. The spectators, press and other golfers began to sense a victory for Jacklin. If he were older and more experienced they would be sure of it. But the pressure of the British Open—as it is with the other three legs of the Grand Slam—is great for both a seasoned pro and especially so for a young player.

Charles began making one final bid on the back nine, gaining strokes at the 10th and 13th holes. Jacklin's vision of victory began to dim a bit. But he held on, with time and holes running out on Charles. By the time they reached the 18th tee, Jacklin clung to a two-stroke lead.

The crowd had swelled by then, stretching down both sides of the fairway and filling two large stands to capacity, with people literally hanging from the rafters. It was close now. Charles hit first and pulled his shot to the righthand side of the fairway, into

Tony Jacklin uses "English" to sink putt.

the rough. Whether Jacklin felt a lessening of tensions then remains unanswered. But his shot was the longest and straightest he had hit during the entire tournament.

Charles played next and sent a beautiful shot to within 18 feet of the pin. It was close enough for Charles to hole the putt and take a three.

The pressure was suddenly back on Jacklin and the all-important second shot. He did not take much time in playing it, either. Tony knew the longer he took, the worse it would be for him. He stepped up and lifted a shot that was even more perfect than Charles'. It landed just four yards from the cup and even as the ball was sailing through the air, the spectators began to cheer the remarkable achievement which was just moments away.

The crowd rushed the greens and engulfed Jacklin. The police herded them back behind the barriers and the unruffled Tony calmly lined up his putt. Every step he took was cheered. Jacklin's 12-foot putt missed, but he had played it safe and was left with a tap-in for his first British Open championship.

Once the ball plunked into the cup, all hell broke loose. Jacklin retrieved the ball and threw it into the crowd. Charles shook his hand and so did the caddies. As he walked off the green, he was greeted by his wife and scores of photographers. Then came the interviews with the press, radio and television.

Finally, it was time for the presentation. The crowds, which usually are bored listening to remarks by tournament officials before the winner is introduced, were even more impatient this time. They wanted Jacklin; they wanted to hear him speak in the accent that would reassure them the British Open belonged to the British again. Many had never witnessed such a sight.

For the staid British, it was a departure from their usual unruffled behavior. Little did they know then that Jacklin would go on to win the U.S. Open that same year, the first Englishman to win that tournament in 50 years. People could identify with him, just as the Americans identified with Palmer.

Jacklin was not born with a golf club in his hands. In fact he was a soccer player in his boyhood days. It wasn't until his 12th birthday that he took up the sport while caddying for his father.

Jacklin is doubtful about this shot.

After the introduction, a love affair ensued. Jacklin would deliver newspapers after school and then rush to the club where he would spend a great deal of time on the course. He practiced and practiced, making himself into a great golfer. When he turned pro, he marched to the top of the golf world and into his countrymen's hearts in the short space of six years.

One of the great disappointments a golfer can face is to have a championship apparently won and then let it slip away. It was like that for Doug Sanders in the 1970 British Open, a tournament which served to prove that Sanders was not washed up—even if he let victory get away.

Doug had long been known as the playboy golfer of the Western world. His exploits on and off the course were well publicized and he did nothing to discourage the image. He was flamboyant—dressing in bright slacks and shirts. While not a long hitter, he was able to produce a great deal of distance from his short, compact swing.

The 1970 event was one of the best Opens. The Royal and Ancient Golf Club invited all surviving past Open winners to a dinner on the eve of the tournament. Sixteen accepted the invitation and big crowds showed up at St. Andrews to witness the event. On the first day of the tournament, play was held up by mist, of all things. In time it cleared and the golfers walked to the first tee.

With just a slight breath of wind blowing, the scores were low during the first round. Neil Coles fired a 65, Tommy Horton a 66, and a score of others were under 70. But once again, most of the talk was about Jacklin. He shot an incredible 29 on the front nine. But while Tony was playing the back nine, a storm blew up and increased in violence. Soon the greens were flooded and play had to be suspended. The officials faced a problem. Should they cancel the entire day's play, or should action resume from the point it was terminated the following day? They decided to resume.

When Jacklin walked on the course the next morning, a stiff breeze greeted him. He did not play well and settled for a 67 for his first round—one that had promised to be a record breaking performance the day before. After shooting a 70 in the afternoon, Tony trailed Trevino by one stroke at the halfway mark. There with Tony was Sanders, well in range of challenging for his first Open title.

Sanders carded a 71 on the third and even more blustery day, keeping him behind Trevino and tied with Jacklin for second. Also making his presence known was Nicklaus, but for one of the few times, eyes were not focused on him.

The last round proved to be disastrous for Trevino and Jacklin. Trevino's score soared to 77. Jacklin appeared tired, perhaps never having recovered from the disappointment of the first day when the storm deprived him of what may have been one of the best rounds in golf history. It was left to Sanders and Nicklaus to

Lee Trevino grimaces as putt misses hole during play in 1972 British Open.

fight it out for first place. On the 17th hole, Sanders played one of the best sand shots of his career and left himself only a foot and a half from the pin. He sank the short putt and took a stroke lead over Nicklaus.

All Sanders needed on the final hole was a par four. He played a good drive, and his pitch shot was eight yards from the flag. Sanders was not taking any chances at that point and sent a conservative putt rolling to the pin. It was short, but only three feet separated Doug from his first Open. He studied the putt at length and then stroked the ball. Three feet, that's all it would take. He missed. The ball faded away to the right and Sanders had to undergo the agony of a playoff the final day. It was to be anti-climactic. He had already lost the British Open.

The sympathy of the spectators could not undo that fateful putt. The St. Andrews course had been the site of many dramatic finishes but perhaps none more dramatic as this one. In the playoff Nicklaus jumped out to a four-stroke lead at the 13th hole and most of the spectators thought the tournament was over. Sanders, however, regained his composure and began a comeback. He birdied the 14th hole and added another at the 15th. He made a par at the 16th while Nicklaus bogeyed that hole. Suddenly he trailed by only one stroke.

After both parred the 17th hole, Nicklaus and Sanders reached the 18th still a stroke apart. Doug drove to within 30 yards of the green while Nicklaus unleashed a drive that carried past the flag. Sanders pitched to within five feet and Nicklaus to within eight. Jack putted first and the ball curved into the hole at the last minute. Sanders stood by helplessly, watching a man win the title he thought was his just 24 hours earlier.

Nicklaus was cast by circumstances into the villain's role, but the Open had never been an easy event for him, either. He had won it for a second time and Sanders had perhaps lost his last opportunity to join the elite.

Nicklaus would go on to suffer his own tragedy in the British Open. Trevino finally mastered the high winds and mist to win in 1971 and then performed a golfing rarity when he made it back-to-back British Opens with a victory in 1972. It came after Nicklaus had won the Masters and U.S. Open and seemed on the verge of becoming the first and only Grand Slam winner since Bobby Jones did it in 1930.

Nicklaus would gladly trade his triumph over Sanders for a victory in 1972. The tournament was held at Muirfield, where Jack had always played well. But the pressure of the Slam had begun to get to him—and this ultimately made the difference against Trevino, a superb golfer who seemingly feels no pressure as he jokes and entertains the gallery during the course of a round.

Lee held a six-stroke lead over Nicklaus as the final round began, but Jack began to fight back, making up strokes so quickly that he even held the lead at the 10th and 11th holes. But the string of birdies ran out and he settled back to play conservative golf the rest of the day. Trevino, meanwhile, holed out a sensational pitch shot on the 17th hole to take a one-stroke lead to the final tee. Perhaps Lee could have played it "safe" at that point. But Lee, much like Arnold Palmer, doesn't wait for a victory to come to him. He goes after it. Trevino reared back and drove the ball to the right of the fairway, only a 7-iron from the green. He made a par-four and won the tournament. Nicklaus played the final hole safely, hoping for Trevino to blunder. He didn't—and Nicklaus' Grand Slam dreams evaported then and there.

To win a tournament like the British Open even once is a landmark. To win it more than once, a golfer must be both lucky and good. But five times? Peter Thompson holds that distinction—a golfer whose reputation was built mostly in Britain and who never really became a big name in the U.S. But not even Nicklaus, Palmer or Trevino can claim five victories in any one major golf tournament.

Despite his monumental British Open victories, Thompson is not the personality the others are. He is not flashy, flamboyant or colorful. Rather, he is calm, methodical in his approach and lacks any degree of showmanship. He answers reporters' questions briskly and technically, leaving the funny lines for others. A deep thinker, Thompson is all concentration on a golf course. It's likely his British Open record will stand for some time to come.

Thompson first became known to the British golfing world when he finished as the runnerup in the 1952 Open. In 1953, he was second to Ben Hogan, firmly establishing himself as a contender for 1954. Bob Locke was the favorite, though. Through the early rounds Thompson trailed and it wasn't until the final day, when one-by-one the contenders failed, that Peter surged into the lead by a stroke. Locke needed a three on the final hole to catch him, but Bobby failed. Thompson, without any fuss or fanfare, had won his first Open. He won his second one at St. Andrews in 1955. The quiet Australian finished with a total of 281, playing steady, if not spectacular, golf. John Fallon was second and Frank Jowle was third.

Thompson's next victory came in 1956 at Hoylake and established his place in golf's record book. He became the first player to record three straight victories since the tournament became one of 72 holes. He defeated competition which included Gary Player, Al Balding, Bruce Crampton and Mike Souchak. It included more international players than any Open up to that time.

The weather was poor but

Bobby Locke of South Africa was 1950 British Open champion.

Thompson seemed unperturbed as he registered opening rounds of 70 and 70 while others chased their golf balls into the sand and rough. Thompson played the wind better than any golfer in the field. The long hitters had difficulty keeping the ball in play. Thompson emerged the winner and yet there were those who still doubted him because he had yet to face the full weight of the American invasion.

Thompson and Locke engaged in another struggle in 1957. Locke, a Sorth African, seemed to sense his days of supremacy were about to end with the emergence of Gary Player. After three rounds Bobby led by three strokes. He held on to win and break Thompson's domination. However, Thompson's turn came again in 1958 at Royal Lytham. After 72 holes, Peter was tied with Englishman Dave Thomas , a close friend. Thompson had tried to convince Thomas to play in the U.S. and develop through competition. But Thomas was content with life in Britain, and in the playoff had to be content with second place. Thompson won by four strokes for his fourth British Open.

Thompson had to wait seven years for his fifth championship. It came in 1965, when Palmer, Nicklaus and Player had turned the Open into an event of great magnitude. The tourney was held at Birkdale and barriers had to be erected to keep the crowds back. Television towers were also set up as the tournament was beamed back to the U.S.

And so, who took control of the tournament? Not the flashy or exciting Palmer, but Thompson, who led after three rounds with his great control of the ball. In conditions that would disturb the best players, Peter was his stoic self. He held a one-stroke lead over the late Tony Lema heading into the final round, with Palmer two strokes in back.

In 1965, 36 holes were played on the final day. Stamina became a factor, and Thompson was clinging to his lead. Lema, who won the year before, was playing as Thompson's partner and both felt one of them would win. Needing nine strokes on the final two holes to win, Thompson finished up in seven to win by two over Roberto De Vicenzo. Lema faded with a final 74.

In succeeding years, the growth and magnitude of the British Open has solidified its hold as part of golf's Grand Slam. Money has increased, but it amounts to just several thousand dollars in American currency and obviously is not the reason why U.S. pros are willing to pack their bags and head overseas.

Australian Peter Thomson won British Open crown five times.

The British Open is now one of the world's sporting spectacles. Enthusiasts from all over attend the event despite the uncomfortable weather that is so much a part of the tournament. Satellites make it possible for Americans to view the final rounds in the comfort of their own homes.

And if any golfer is to win the Grand Slam, he'll now have to do it in front of millions in each of the four events. The Masters, U.S. Open, P.G.A. and British Open—four tests of a champion. Can anyone win all four in one year? The odds are against it. It's difficult enough merely winning one in a lifetime. ■

THE PGA SCHOOL

TEE SHOTS AND TAXES

■ Don't be surprised if one of these days a pro golfer reaches into his bag for a 6-iron and comes out with a book describing the finer points of club fitting or one giving six easy ways to make an acceptance speech after winning a tournament. Knowing how to do both is as important as being able to break par if a golfer wants to join the Professional Golfers Association.

Of the dozens of pros who participate on the tour, most are members of the P.G.A. Some, however, have qualified to play under the guidelines of the Approved Players Tournament Division, but cannot take part in the annual PGA championship. Neither can they qualify for the Vardon Trophy—which is awarded to the player with the lowest

Touring pro Hale Irwin completed his studies at the PGA Schools in 1972.

Veteran pros like Dave Marr (top) and Bob Goalby do so well on tour that they don't have time for school.

average when the year is completed. Nor can they represent the U.S. on the Ryder Cup team. And they would have difficulty developing into good club pros without becoming PGA members.

For the college graduate who may have played four years of golf on scholarship, the PGA Business Schools can be compared to post-graduate studies which others take to earn a Masters. For those players who haven't gone to college, or who did several years ago, it's back to school again.

There are 10 PGA schools located around the country. They are geographically placed to lower the cost for a player who wants to become a member but can't afford to travel to the two schools in Palm Beach Gardens, Fla., headquarters for the entire PGA operation. The schools are divided into two classes—School I, which is basically a classroom course, and School II which enables the golfers to put some of what they have learned to use.

The object of the schools is to make a player a better all-around golfer. When he graduates he will know more about club fitting, public relations and speaking, course design and maintenance and the financial aspect of the game. He'll know what to do with those big purses that are available almost every week of the year.

"Our schools now have an enrollment of about 1,500," says Gary Wiren, director of education for the PGA. "Most of them are primarily younger men new to the business, but about 20 per cent

Big winners like Lanny Wadkins learn how to handle and invest their money.

are guys over 40 who never attempted to become PGA members and now have decided they want to." There are six schools grouped in Division I and they're located in Buffalo, Kansas City, Mo., Atlantic City, N.J., San Francisco, Louisville and Palm Beach Gardens.

"It's a five-day concentrated course with a total of 33 hours of classes," Wiren says. "The subjects range from public relations, to health courses, taxes, course design and repairing clubs. We try to utilize successful PGA members as teachers and we also bring in accountants and sales people to lecture about finances. The classes start at 8:30 a.m. and finish at 9:30 p.m. The players complain that they're too long."

The temptation to walk out and hit several balls off the tee during lunch must be great. But Wiren says playing 18 holes is not a part of the school procedure. The players are there to increase their knowledge of the game from every possible angle. "It's to develop their skills and knowledge," he points out.

Players such as Bob Murphy and Hale Irwin completed their "educations" in 1972, though both were successful tour players several years earlier. "Guys like Jack Nicklaus went to the school, but that was when we only had the school I set up," Wiren states. "Those schools were started in 1967. Now we have the new concept with two school divisions and we also added an apprentice program in 1970. There was so much information, we had to expand."

The sight of Nicklaus sitting in a classroom and learning how to replace divots would probably amuse even the most stoic pro. But the PGA claims it wants its golfers

PGA Schools teach pros all about course design and course maintainence.

to know more than what club to use to hit a ball out of a sand trap. Finances for example, have become increasingly more important since the 1940s. Golf is big business now.

A player must know what tax bracket he belongs in—and this fluctuates with the amount of money he wins each year. His costs for playing the tour can amount to $25,000 or more and at one time that figure would have topped the money-winning lists. Golfers also must know how to work out agreements when endorsing golf balls and clubs and when they are asked to do radio or television commercials for other products. There is also the

matter of how much of a fee to ask for at a speaking engagement. It's all more difficult to keep track of since the income is never fixed. Many of the younger players just out of college have become big winners on the tour. A player such as Lanny Watkins won over $100,000 as a rookie in 1972. By attending the PGA schools he would, theoretically, be better able to handle his newfound wealth.

The School I part of the program is the most difficult. When the five days are up, each student is given an exam that Wiren calls "hard." A year later the players must enroll in School II to complete the required courses.

Those schools number four and are located in Pinehurst, Palm Beach Gardens, Houston and San Marcos, Calif. It's at these sites that the golfers finally get to work outdoors. The course is primarily concerned with teaching a player to teach others. Qualified pros instruct players on how to go about instructing beginners—which is especially vital if that player wants to eventually become a club pro.

"They are working outdoors on a tee," Wiren explains. "They're not in hotel rooms all day listening to instructors. But all of it is important because a golfer has to be pretty smooth. He's got to be an athlete, salesman, public relations man, teacher, craftsman and maintenance man."

The School II operation is the more recent of the two. As Wiren

Ken Still received some of the top marks on record in the PGA Schools.

Portly Bob Murphy was one of young pros who got his "degree" last year.

mentioned, one cram course was not enough. When too much information is fed to a player all at once, he will tend merely to memorize it so he can pass the exam. Little of it will be retained.

After completing his course in School II a student is subjected to another exam. "It's an oral one and a written one," Wiren says. "He has to pass it to qualify for membership."

But in setting up its rules for PGA members, the organization did not overlook the most important qualification—and that is the ability to play. Even after passing the exams a player must earn 32

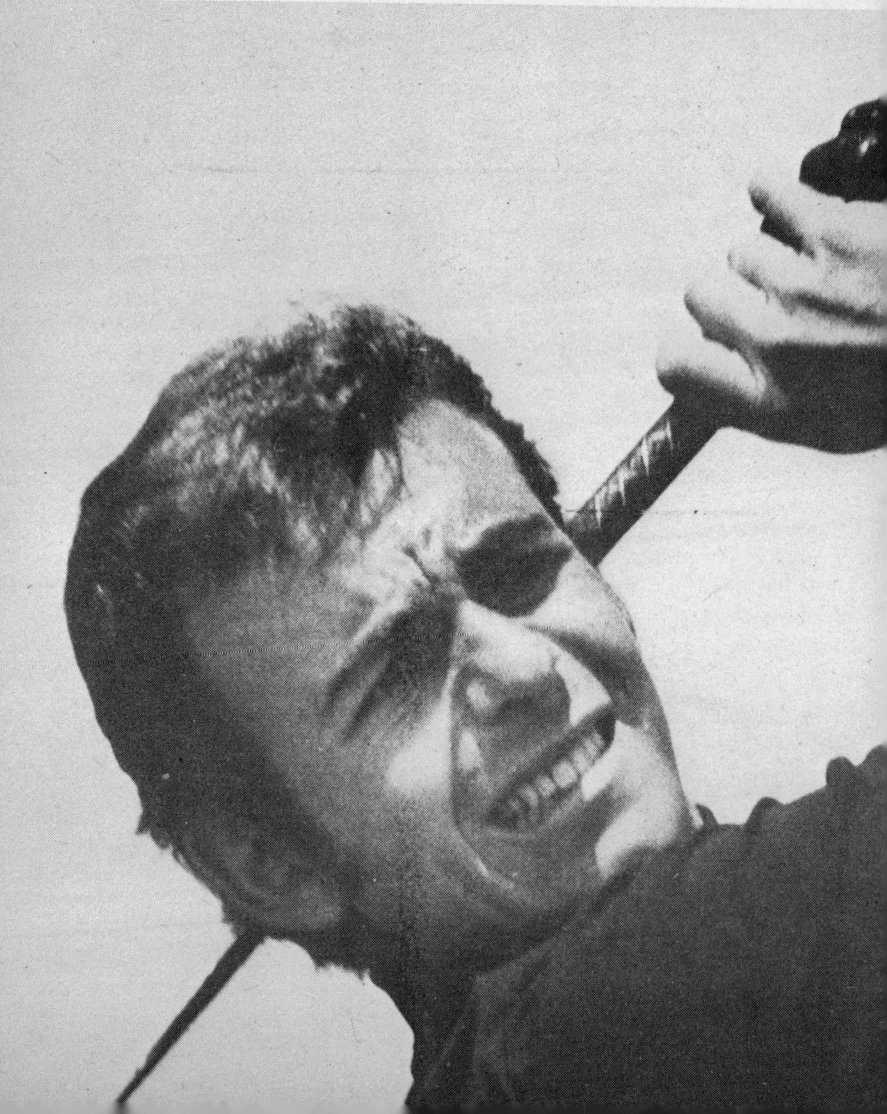

credits before becoming a member of the PGA.

"They can qualify for that in one of two ways," Wiren comments. "They can work in a golf shop or make it by playing on the tour."

Working in a pro shop would earn a PGA applicant one credit, and then that would multiply with the number of months he spends there. In a couple of years he would earn the required 32 credits to become a member.

In golf shops employees learn more about equipment and the makeup of a course. However, most pros worked in shops at one time or another. Many start in their early teens when they caddy for weekend golfers on public courses. They move to club courses where they continue to work as caddies. Eventually, they work inside the shops, servicing pros and club members.

It all requires a thorough knowledge of golf. A shop offers everything from clubs to tees to caps, sweaters and jackets. Many of those who work in shops never participate on the pro tour. Some merely compete in local tournaments. Eventually they become club pros.

The golfer whose game is good enough to make the pro tour doesn't have it easier, however, as he attempts to earn his 32 credits. For the playing pros, it means qualifying for a tournament on Monday, then making the 36-hole cut once it starts. A player receives a half credit for every cut he makes in a PGA event. He receives one credit per cut, if he is already an established member of the tour who is not subjected to qualifying every Monday. "It takes something like 64 events to gain the number of credits necessary," Wiren says.

That remains as the most diffi-

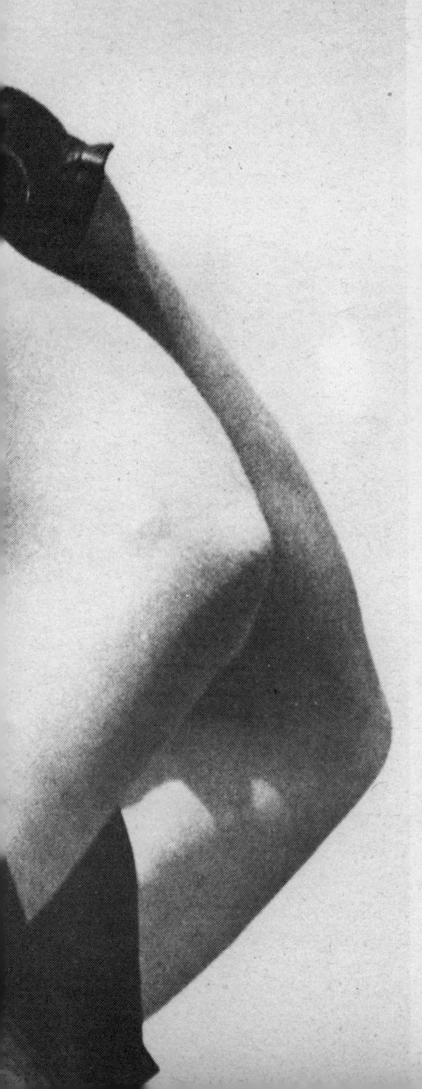

Tony Jacklin learned the hard way—hanging around the pro shop.

cult part of any pro golfer's life. Once a player has become exempt, he no longer must sweat it out with a hundred others on the Monday before a tournament. He knows where his next stop will be and can use the time to travel and practice. He can also probably reach the goal of 32 credits within a shorter period of time.

But players who tee up on Monday have to be at their best merely to beat out the competition for those few remaining openings in the tournament field. Often a player will not be at his best once the tourney starts and he'll miss the cut. It means he hasn't earned his half-credit and must suffer through the same procedure the following week. In these instances most fellows tend to forget about becoming PGA members and worry more about how they're going to meet their expenses.

There are some aspiring golfers who never get that far. "There are 37 section committees in the country and they usually request that a potential member has had a handicap of six or has at least broken 80," Wiren explains. "The PGA is not going to allow just anyone to tee up in a tournament."

With everything taken into consideration the PGA estimates that it requires a minimum of 40 months before a player has completed his courses at the schools and earned enough credits to become a member. Those who have attended college, are given eight credits to start with. It means they have to earn only 24 before qualifying.

The increase in golf scholarships given by colleges today is one of the reasons the golf school concept became a necessity. More and more young athletes turned to the sport because of its get-rich-quick appeal. With a heavy influx of young players on the tour, the PGA felt that further education was needed in order to maintain the professionalism of the sport.

Just 10 and 15 years ago, the game was dominated by a handful of players, and most of the faces on the tour were familiar. Now every tournament will usually unveil a new face—new to the public and most of the pros, too. The school will make the PGA feel better about the pros who represent them. However, Wiren doesn't think the present setup is the ideal one.

"It's not a finalized idea yet," he says. "We're trying to eventually make them do the operation instead of listening to it." He feels the players will retain more and become better educated if they can learn about things such as club fitting by doing them rather than sitting through an hour lecture. "That's our goal now," Wiren states. "But we still have six hours of studying rules that won't change."

Eventually, the PGA hopes its members will all be as knowledgeable about the game as any teaching pro. They'll be able to cut the greens, fix a club head, speak eloquently in front of father-son dinners and explain how to shoot a 69 on any course in the country.

Then, of course, they must walk out to the first tee and do it. ■

SPORTSCOPE®

A Sports-fan 'Bonus'

Sportsfacts & Highlights

Great Moments in Sports

Full-Color Action Photos

Sports Reviews

Gift Product Catalogue

Published by Sport-Scope®, Inc. New York, N.Y.

SPORT-SCOPE FORUM

Do you have any pertinent, amusing, informative or just plain interesting ideas on the world of sports? Just drop us a note, and the editors of SPORT-SCOPE will pass on the most timeless nuggets to our eager sportsfans. Here's one from Irv Solarchik of Matawan, N.J.:

"Why isn't there a 20-second time limit for pitchers? There's nothing more boring than to watch a pitcher go through his routine of twitching and scratching before he releases the ball . . . probably 15 to 20 minutes of no-action nonsense would be cut from every game . . ."

Any opinions, pro or con? Write to:

SPORT-SCOPE FORUM
180 Madison Avenue
New York, N.Y. 10016

SPORTS ON TV

Did you know that in the last 12 years the number of TV hours devoted to sports has doubled? In 1960, about 7½% of network TV consisted of sports programming, while today each of the three networks allocates 15% of its annual schedule to sports coverage.

And what do you suppose was the highest-rated program of all in 1972? None other than "Super Bowl VI," which out-rated such programs as "Love Story" (the movie), and Bob Hope's "Christmas Show."

MEMORABLE MOMENTS OF PRO BASKETBALL

Lifted to greatness by rookies Bill Russell and Tom Heinsohn, the 1956-57 Boston Celtics have come down to the wire in their final playoff match with the St. Louis Hawks. With the series tied 3-3, the deciding game is being played before 13,909 fans in Boston Garden. With six seconds to go in regulation, the great Bob Pettit of St. Louis sinks two free throws, and it's 103-103: overtime. Boston's Bill Sharman misses a jumper at the buzzer, and it's 113-113 and another overtime. Finally, Boston's Frank Ramsey breaks a 121-121 tie, and the Celtics hold on for a 125-123 victory—their first playoff win, but certainly not the last.

ANGLING FOR BUSINESS

Incredible, but true—well over $5-billion was spent last year by sport fishermen! This includes expenditures for goods and services directly relating to angling. And according to a U.S. government report, in the period between 1960 and 1970, "habitual anglers"—those who fished at least three days a year in either salt or fresh water — increased by 31 per cent to 33,158,000. The figures for 1972, not yet available, should go higher.

Two more fishing facts gleaned from the report:

1. In 1970 the average salt-water angler spent $10.77 a day to go fishing. His fresh-water counterpart spent $6.30.

2. In 1970 those anglers who fished salt water exclusively were outnumbered, 8 to 1, by those who spent all their time on fresh water.

MEMORABLE MOMENTS IN BASEBALL

Ed Walsh's loss to Addie Joss (1-0 no-hitter) after 40 straight wins, Oct. 2, 1908.

Sept. 6, 1883, Tommy Burns gets three extra-base hits in one inning.

Lew Burdette beats Yanks for third time in same Series, Oct. 10, 1957.

Alexander fans Tony Lazzeri to win series game for Cards, Oct. 10, 1926.

Oct. 12, 1923, Casey Stengel's homer for Giants tops Yanks, 1-0, in Series.

SPORT-SCOPE MINI-REVIEW

"SEMI-TOUGH," a humorous, hard-hitting and rough (the language, that is) probe into the private lives of pro football players, is a best-selling novel by Sports Illustrated writer Dan Jenkins. This somewhat cynical glimpse inside and outside the locker room is about as penetrating as is possible in the carefully guarded world of professional football. It's not for small-fry readers, so let's call "Semi-Tough" semi-must reading for sports fans.

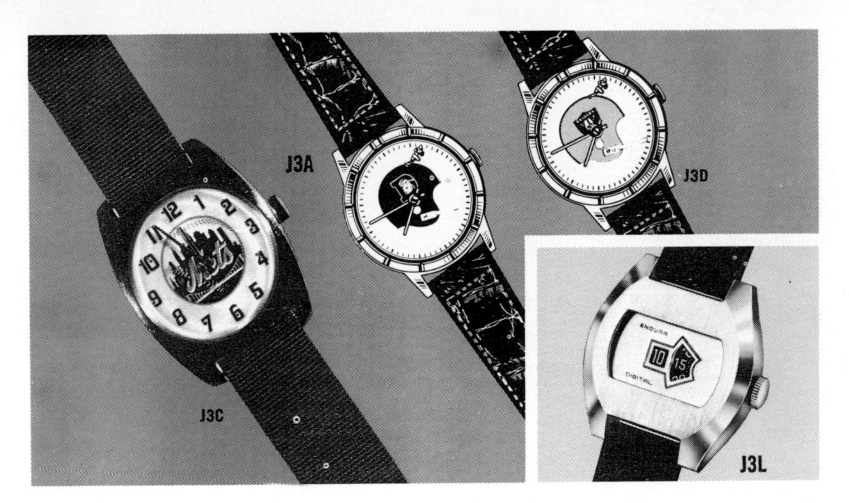

Time and Your NFL Team on Your Wrist!— All Pro Watches. Precision made imported Swiss Lafayette watch, shock resistant, anti-magnetic movement in beautiful gold color case with brown imitation alligator band. Guaranteed. Unique conversation timepiece featuring full color official helmet design of the **team of your choice** . . . with a running player who ticks off the seconds and scores a touchdown with everyone who watches. **J3A $19.95**

Or put time and your favorite Baseball Team on your wrist. **J3C $16.95**

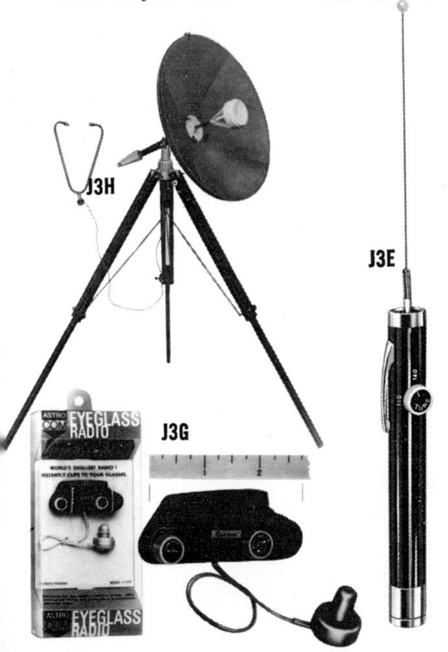

Fabulous Digital Watch — The beautiful "Endura" precision Swiss made digital watch flashes hour and minutes for instant direct digital reading. Ultra modern space-age burnished gold or silver metal. Also select plain or fancy color band.

Ladies J3L Masculine Size J3B $19.95

Endura Wrist Alarm Watch — Set it to to get you to the game on time. Swiss precision movement. Loud insistent alarm. Handsome face — in either gold or silver case. **J3D $18.95**

Big Ear "Electronic Sound Collector" . . . with Stethoscope — "Home-in" for intimate listening on faint sounds 100 feet away or 200 feet away over water. Use indoors or outdoors — baby sitting to bird calls! 100 hours on standard 9 volt battery (not supplied). Complete with sturdy adjustable tripod legs. **J3H $24.95**

Plug in Accessory to broadcast "Big Ear" through your FM Receiver. **J3J $14.95**

The Eyeglass Radio — that you clip onto your glasses. Only 2¾ inches long. With five transistors, picks up all local AM stations. Includes two batteries and hearing aid plug. **J3G $19.95**

Wrist Broadcaster — Broadcast your voice over any FM radio within 50′ **J3M $14.95**

Hear Pilots on "Sky Spy"—Miniature aircraft radio lets you hear what pilots and control tower are saying about arrivals, delays, weather. Miniature radio about size of a pen. Solid state circuitry brings in VHF airplane broadcasts within 15 miles of airplane or tower. Complete with two 1.5V silver oxide hearing aid batteries, pretuned own antenna, and high quality magnetic earphone. **J3E $19.95**

"Super-Spy" — includes leather case, folding antenna, and 20% better range. Ear cord and plug separate for easier packing, saves batteries. **J3F $24.95**

Add Stethoscope for Binocular Hearing for either "Spy." **J3K $3.00**

FREE! Any two 75¢ books free with an order of $10 or more.

Arnie Swings

Still "Mr. Charisma" of the pro golf tour, Arnie Palmer drives a long one down the fairway.

Tennis

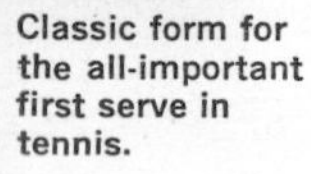

Classic form for the all-important first serve in tennis.

777—Extra Point (Football)

Who says the extra point is automatic? In this great action shot, the "automatic" PAT is about to be blocked.

782—Watkins Glen

On the track at Watkins Glen, N.Y.

ALL PHOTOS ON THESE PAGES WITH CODE NUMBERS ARE AVAILABLE AS 2′ x 3′ POSTERS.

Sailing

Just a pretty scene of a sailboat on the open sea.

1H1—Bobby Orr

Though out of action in '72, the Bruins' Bobby Orr is still rated as the top hockey player of this era.

8B1—Kareem Abdul-Jabbar

Kareem Abdul-Jabbar of the Milwaukee Bucks is one of the great stars of pro basketball.

6N2—Willie Mays

A sure-fire Hall-of-Famer of not so distant future: Willie Mays.

SEE DETAILS ON NEXT PAGE.

SPORTS POSTER BONANZA!

6A89—Otis Taylor

3B1—John Havlicek

8A12—Joe Namath

11N30—Ron Johnson

15N18—Gene Washington

12B1—Elvin Hayes

1B1—Pete Maravich

5N12—Roger Staubach

16N43—Larry Brown

095—Dallas Cowboys

81AL2—All Sports

Sport-Scope brings you over **200** individual 2′ x 3′ full color posters!

You can select from 90 individual sports stars in Football, Basketball, Hockey, Baseball (plus life size hero posters 2′ x 6′ — for Mark Spitz and Joe Frazier). Plus all-color Action Sports. Plus the Big Ten and Notre Dame! Plus over 100 team posters for every major Pro Football, Baseball, Basketball and Hockey Club in the U.S.!

Any 1	3	6	10
$2.00	$5.25	$10.00	$16.00

You will find small illustrations of some of these big color posters on these pages as well as color illustrations on pages 4-D, 5-E, and 16-P. We can fill your order for any of the posters listed, as well as for any U.S. pro team. Simply select the players, the sports, the teams you wish and circle their numbers on the order envelope attached.

ALL POSTERS ARE IN FULL COLOR — ALL POSTERS 2′ x 3′ in size (except for heroic size Joe Frazier and Mark Spitz — which are 2′ x 6′).

FREE! Any two 75¢ books free with an order of $10 or more.

4016—Joe Frazier

765—Hill Climb

778—Cycle Drags

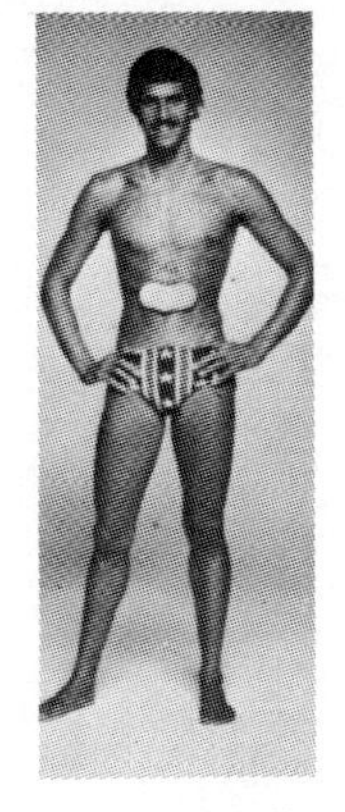

4022—Mark Spitz

CTION SPORTS
747 Pipeline
759 Sky Diving
761 Football
765 Hill Climb
766 Ski Jump
771 Moto Cross
777 Extra Point
778 Cycle Drags
780 Globetrotters
781 Grand Prix (Racing)
782 Watkins Glen

NDIVIDUAL PRO STARS

OOTBALL
1N60 Tommy Nobis
2N32 Mike Curtis
2N36 Norm Bulaich
2N41 Tom Matte
3N40 Gale Sayers
S3N51 Dick Butkus
4N44 Leroy Kelly
4N76 Bill Nelsen
5N12 Roger Staubach
5N14 Craig Morton
5N22 Bob Hayes
5N74 Bob Lilly
6N11 Greg Landry
6N20 Lem Barney
6N24 Mel Farr
7N15 Bart Starr
7N42 J. Brockington
7N66 R. Nitschke
8N18 R. Gabriel
S8N18 R. Gabriel
8N74 Merlin Olsen
9N30 Bill Brown
9N81 Carl Eller
9N84 G. Washington
9N88 Alan Page
10N8 Archie Manning
11N30 Ron Johnson
11N43 Spider Lockhart
12N18 Ben Hawkins
13N34 Andy Russell
13N75 Joe Greene
14N8 Larry Wilson
14N25 Jim Bacon
14N81 Jackie Smith
15N12 John Brodie
15N18 Gene Washington
16N9 Sonny Jurgensen
16N42 Charlie Taylor
16N43 Larry Brown
1A16 Jim Plunkett
1A34 Ron Sellers
2A16 Dennis Shaw
2A36 O.J. Simpson
3A11 Virgil Carter
4A87 Rick Jackson
5A90 George Webster
6A16 Len Dawson
6A89 Otis Taylor
7A12 Bob Griese
7A39 Larry Csonka
7A42 Paul Warfield
8A12 Joe Namath
S8A12 Joe Namath
8A13 Don Maynard
9A16 George Blanda
9A25 F. Biletnikoff
9A40 P. Banaszak
10A21 John Hadl

BASKETBALL
1B1 Pete Maravich
3B1 John Havlicek
6B1 Bob Lanier
7B1 Wilt Chamberlain
7B2 Jerry West
8B1 Kareem Abdul-Jabbar
8B2 Oscar Robertson
9B2 Walt Frazier
9B3 Willis Reed
10B1 B. Cunningham
12B1 Elvin Hayes
13B1 Nate Thurmond

HOCKEY
1H1 Bobby Orr
1H2 Phil Esposito
7H1 Ed Giacomin

BASEBALL
3N4 John Bench
6N2 Willie Mays

HEROIC SIZE (2′ x 6′)
4016 Joe Frazier
4022 Mark Spitz

Your Choice
200 Different
Pro Team Posters

FOOTBALL—AMER
080 Baltimore Colts
081 Buffalo Bills
082 Cinci Bengals
083 Cleveland Browns
084 Denver Broncos
085 Houston Oilers
086 Kansas C. Chiefs
087 Miami Dolphins
088 New Eng. Patriots
089 New York Jets
090 Oakland Raiders
091 Pitts. Steelers
092 S. Diego Chargers

FOOTBALL—NATL
093 Atlanta Falcons
094 Chicago Bears
095 Dallas Cowboys
096 Detroit Lions
097 Green Bay Packers
098 L.A. Rams
099 Minnesota Vikings
100 New Orl'ns Saints
101 N.Y. Giants
102 Phila. Eagles
103 St. L. Cardinals
104 San Fran. 49ers
105 Wash'ton Redskins

BASEBALL—AMER
001 Baltimore Orioles
002 Boston Red Sox
003 California Angels
004 Chicago White Sox
005 Cleveland Indians
006 Detroit Tigers
007 Kansas C. Royals
008 Milwaukee Brewers
009 Minnesota Twins
010 New York Yankees
011 Oakland A's
012 Texas Rangers

BASEBALL—NATL
013 Atlanta Braves
014 Chicago Cubs
015 Cincinnati Reds
016 Houston Astros
017 L.A. Dodgers
018 Montreal Expos
019 New York Mets
020 Phila. Phillies
021 Pitts. Pirates
022 San Diego Padres
023 San Fran. Giants
024 St. L. Cardinals

BASKETBALL—ABA
025 Carolina Cougars
026 Dallas Chaparells
027 Denver Rockets
028 Indiana Pacers
029 Kentucky Colonels
030 Memphis Tams
031 N.Y. Nets
032 S.D. Conquistadors
033 Utah Stars
034 Virginia Squires

BASKETBALL—NBA
035 Atlanta Hawks
036 Baltimore Bullets
037 Boston Celtics
038 Buffalo Braves
039 Chicago Bulls
040 Cleve Cavaliers
041 Detroit Pistons
042 Houston Rockets
043 Kansas C. Royals
044 L.A. Lakers
045 Milwaukee Bucks
046 N.Y. Knicks
047 Phila. 76ers
048 Phoenix Suns
049 Ptld Trailblazers
050 S.F. Warriors
051 Seattle Supersonics

HOCKEY—NHL EAST
052 Boston Bruins
053 Buffalo Sabres
054 Detroit Red Wings
055 M'treal Canadiens
056 N.Y. Islanders
057 N.Y. Rangers
058 Toronto M'pl Leafs
059 Vancouver Canucks

HOCKEY—NHL WEST
060 Atlanta Flames
061 Cal. Golden Seals
062 Chicago Blk Hawks
063 L.A. Kings
064 Minn. North Stars
065 Phila Flyers
066 Pitts. Penguins
067 St. Louis Blues

HOCKEY—WORLD
068 Alberta Oilers
069 Chicago Cougars
070 Cleveld Crusaders
071 Houston Aeros
072 L.A. Sharks
073 Minn. Fight Saints
074 New Engld Whalers
075 N.Y. Raiders
076 Ottawa Nationals
077 Phila Blazers
078 Quebec Nordiques
079 Winnipeg Jets

Big Ten Colleges
201 Illinois
202 Indiana
203 Iowa
204 Michigan
205 Michigan State
206 Minnesota
207 Northwestern
208 Ohio State
209 Purdue
210 Wisconsin
211 + Notre Dame

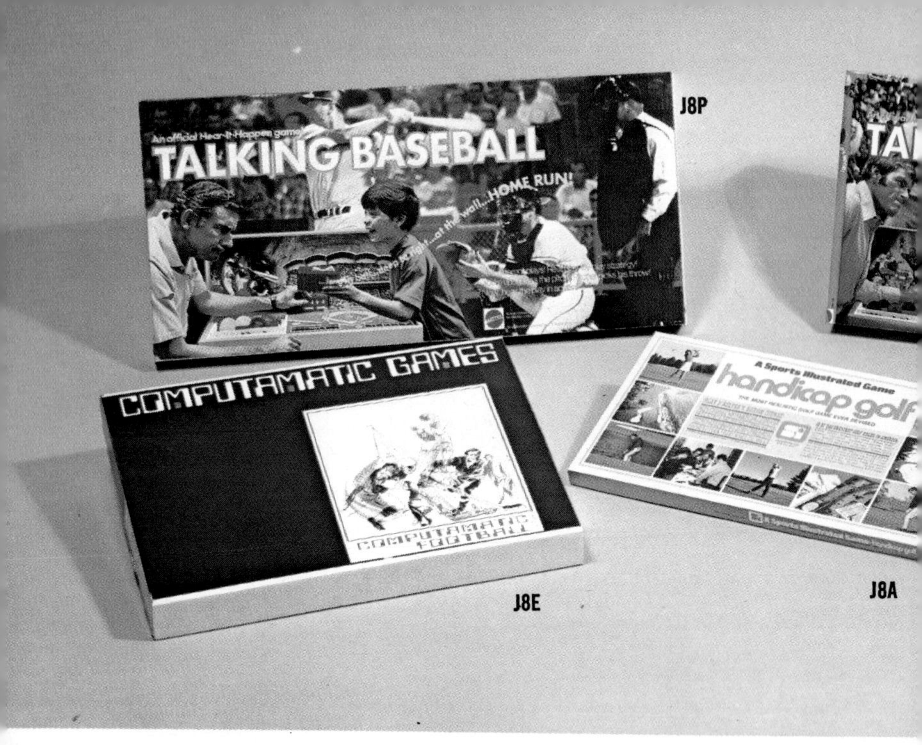

MATTEL'S "TALKING BASEBALL" . . . Lets pitcher call his pitch, batter guess it, both teams make strategic moves in every possible game situation — 274 different plays in all. Hit-and-run, pitchout, steal — you call it! Then hear the play in action! Game includes automatic sportscaster (operated by 1 "D" battery, not included), 12 records, record rack, spin-dial scoreboard, player pegs, diamond, score sheets. **J8P $11.95**

MATTEL'S "TALKING FOOTBALL." You're the quarterback — for as long as you can move the ball . . . or you're the defensive captain — until you stop the other team. One player calls the play, opponent calls defensive signals. Then . . . you hear the actual play, broadcast! Game includes automatic sportscaster (operated by 1 "D" battery, not included) 13 records, record rack, spin-dial scoreboard, playing field, field markers, goal posts, moving football. **J8O $11.95**

ADVANTAGE HOCKEY. The board game of strategy with all the high-speed action and excitement of the real thing. **J8N $7.00**

SPORTS ILLUSTRATED HANDICAP GOLF. Pit your handicap against 18 of America's classic great golf holes — from the first at Merion to the 18th at Pebble Beach! Game includes eight individual handicap charts (from Scratch to Duffer), distance and direction indicator, playing boards featuring magnificent color layouts of each hole, complete rules, plus a "caddy" with tips on playing each hole. Tour course in just 30 minutes—with no greens fee! **J8A $9.45**

SPORTS ILLUSTRATED PRO FOOTBALL. Can you come up with the right game plan and plays to use your squad's skills? Fascinating realistic strategy game. **J8B $9.45**

SPORTS ILLUSTRATED COLLEGE FOOTBALL. You be the coach! Use your head and football know-how to get the most from each of 32 top teams of last decade. **J8C $9.45**

SPORTS ILLUSTRATED MAJOR LEAGUE BASEBALL. You manage 24 teams, 600 players (everyone from Aaron to Yaz) . . . and call everything from batting order to steals. 9 inning game—30 minutes. **J8D $9.45**

FREE! Any two 75¢ books free with an order of $10 or more.

COMPUTER FOOTBALL. The Thinking Fan's action game. You secretly call your play — pass, run, kick, field goal, fake kick . . . anything — your opponent tries to outsmart you and stop the play. The computamatic board instantly flashes the computed results. Exciting, challenging, strategic, realistic. Success is based as in football and life on skill, strategy and luck. And — you can use the same football console for five other equally challenging games. Add game changing overlays. **J8E $34.95**

(To Change Console) — Overlay Only		
COMPUTAMATIC HOCKEY	J9F	$9.95
COMPUTAMATIC BASEBALL	J9G	$9.95
COMPUTAMATIC SOCCER	J9H	$9.95
COMPUTAMATIC GOLF	J9J	$9.95
COMPUTAMATIC SAILING (for 4)	J9K	$9.95

ADVANTAGE TENNIS . . . the board game that lets you perfect your tennis strategy. Beginners learn fundamentals; advanced players learn advanced tactics. You place your serve, drive, and volley . . . set up your next shot . . . force your opponent into errors. . . . You learn how to play net, how to cover court, how to hit and return shots for winners from every position. Keep score by point, game, and set — even tie-breakers. Rule booklet, illustrated shots, court diagrams. Instructions included. **J8L $7.00**

ADVANTAGE BASKETBALL. The strategy, action, excitement, and all options of real basketball, in a fascinating game. **J8M $7.00**

NFL ELECTRIC FOOTBALL 635 . . . WITH TOTAL TEAM CONTROL. Now you control all 22 men and every move they make. Officially sanctioned by NFL. For first time you can run real NFL plays. Complete with set of easy-to-apply numbers so you can spot your favorite NFL stars in action. Realistic moulded figures. Colorful steel gameboard. NFL gold goal posts, adjustable score board, moveable chain marker, patented timer, two quarterbacks that pass, kick, run, fumble actual miniature footballs. **J8Q $15.00**

NFL Electric Football (without Team Control)	J8R	$10.00
Official Major League Baseball	J8S	$10.00
NFL Strategy, with Official NFL Playbook	J8T	$20.00
Tudor Players Hockey— Live Puck Action you control	J8V	$13.50
Larger-with Scoreboard	J8W	$24.50
With Sturdy Aluminum Legs	J8X	$30.00

FREE! Any two 75¢ books free with an order of $10 or more.

VOLTMETER. Now, right from the driver's seat, check your car's electrical system — battery, voltage regulator, and generator (or alternator) — with one precision instrument! Just plug this solid state tester into cigarette lighter socket . . . and find out what's what in seconds — Color-coded dial is accurate within 2%. Simple instructions on case, can't get lost. **J10E $8.95**

PRECISION AUTO AND BOAT COMPASS. Handsome, luminous safe dial (approved by the A.E.C.), for nighttime reading. Swivel-mounted for all-angle viewings. Optional suction cup or adhesive disc mountings included. Geared compensators permit precision adjustment with tool supplied. Fully chrome plated body; internal damping device to reduce dial surging when you corner, accelerate, or brake. Installation and adjusting instructions included. **J10A $5.95**

SUPER SPORT COMPASS. Mounts on windshield or dash with super suction cup. Ball joint permits easy tilting for all angle viewing. Sports luminous dial of safe material approved by Atomic Energy Commission. Fingertip controls adjust magnetic compensators easily and precisely — no adjusting tools needed. Advanced hydraulic type. Installation and adjusting instructions. Choose black, beige or red. **J10B $4.75**

PROFESSIONAL TIRE GAUGE. You bet your life on tire pressure — just as race drivers do. So use this rugged precision instrument (comes with a written Guarantee of Accuracy). Inflate your tires to exact pressure . . . improve your car's steering, handling, cornering, braking, tire life — even gas mileage! Precision bronze bourdon tube with full-geared solid brass movement. Easy-to-read 0 to 60 lb. dial, heavy steel case, polished unbreakable crystal. **J10C $3.25**

WIDE ANGLE REAR VIEW MIRROR. Greater visibility and safety—full 170° panoramic rear view eliminates blind spots! 20" long mirror utilizes 3 panels of shatterproof, non-glare glass to provide 300% more vision . . . without distortion! Approved for cars, trucks, buses — (meets Nat. Bur. of Stan.); also meets Marine Water Skiing requirements for all states. Complete with mounting kit and instructions. **J10D $9.50**

INFLATABLE, SELF-VENTILATING BUCKET SEAT. Lets you ride in cool comfort and ease, on a cushion of air! Inflates easily in seconds. Tough heavy-duty vinyl construction, rich leather look! Lessens driver fatigue . . . no backache in the stadium . . . less tiring fishing . . . a softer life on a camping trip. Relax in comfort. 17" x 17", with 17" high back. **J10F 2 for $4.95**

FREE! Any two 75¢ books free with an order of $10 or more.

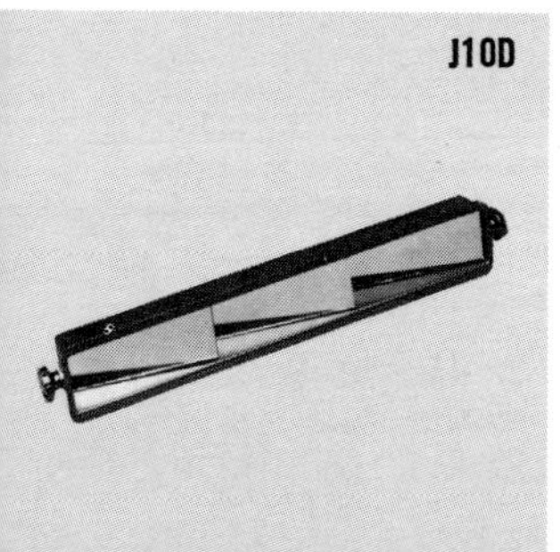
J10D

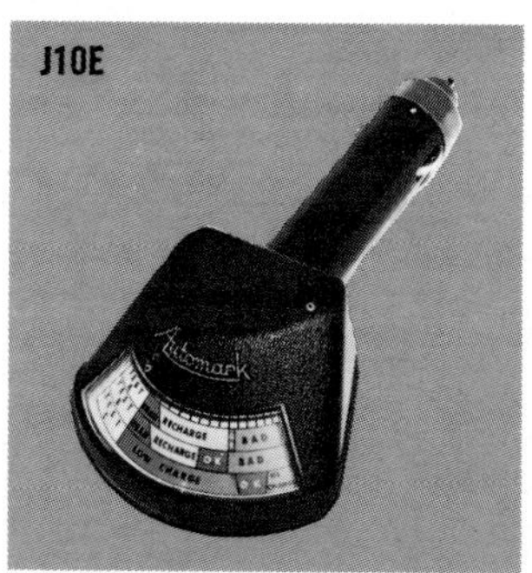

J10E

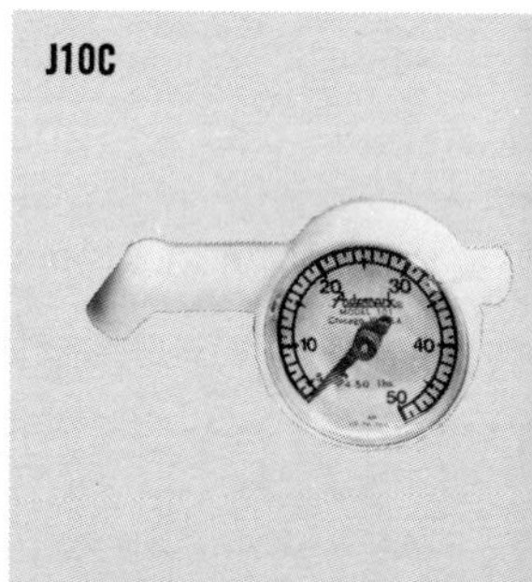

J10C

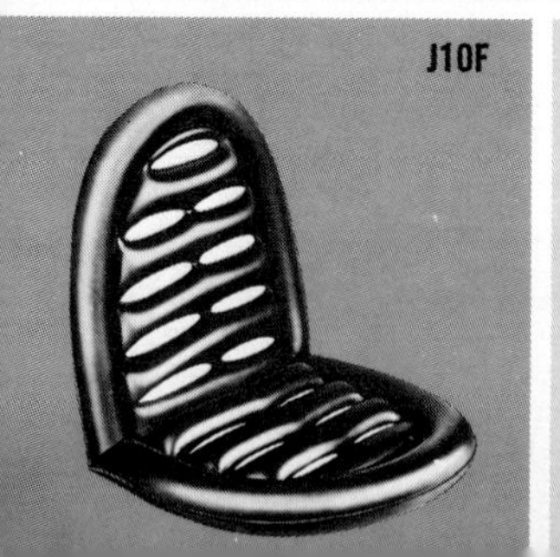
J10F

J10B

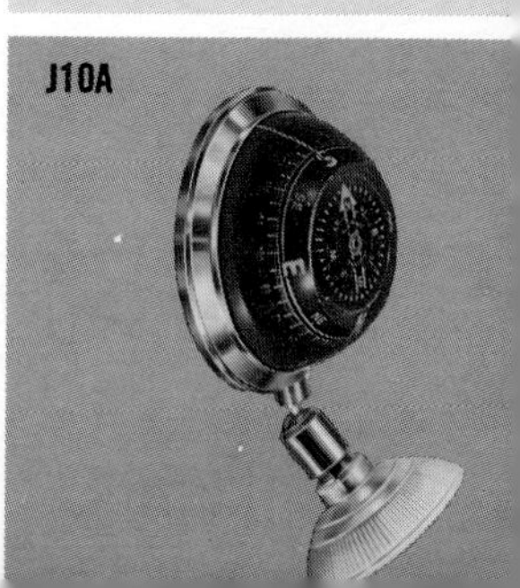
J10A

BUILD YOUR OWN **SPORTSBOOK LIBRARY** WITH THESE GREAT TITLES FROM STADIA

PRO FOOTBALL

			Price
11AL0	Illus. Digest of Pro Football	1970	$1.50
11AL1	Illus. Digest of Pro Football	1971	1.50
11AL2	Illus. Digest of Pro Football	1972	1.50
11BS1	Super Bowl	1971	.75
11BL2	Super Bowl	1972	1.50
11CL2	Inside Pro Football	1972	1.50
11DS2	You Are The Running Back	1972	.60
11ES2	You Are The Quarterback	1972	.60
62AL2	Pro Quarterback Handbook	1972	1.95

BASEBALL

14AL1	Illus. Digest of Baseball	1971	$1.50
14AL2	Illus. Digest of Baseball	1972	1.50
14BS1	World Series	1971	.75
14BS2	World Series	1972	.75
14CS2	The Glory Years of Baseball	1972	.75

GOLF

42AS2	Golf's Big 3	1972	.75
42BL3	Grand Slam	1973	1.50

RACING

51AS2	Big 4 of American Auto Racing	1972	.75
51BL3	The Glory Road	1973	1.50
52AS2	The Triple Crown of Horse Racing	1972	.75

PRO BASKETBALL

12AL1	Illus. Digest of Pro Basketball	1971	$1.50
12AL2	Illus. Digest of Pro Basketball	1972-3	1.50
12BS2	One on One	1972	.75
12BL3	One on One	1973	1.50
12CS2	NBA ABA Playoff	1972	.75
12CL3	Playoff	1973	1.50

HOCKEY

13AL2	Illus. Digest of Pro Hockey	1972	$1.50
13BS2	Stanley Cup	1972	.75
13BL3	Stanley Cup	1973	1.50

TENNIS

41AL3	Game! Set! Match!	1973	$1.50

BOATING • CAMPING • FISHING

34AL3	Family Book of Boating	1973	1.50
33AL3	Family Book of Camping	1973	1.50
31AL3	Fishing All Waters	1973	1.50

GENERAL

15BS2	The Great Olympians	1972	.75
15AL2	MVP! The Super Pros	1972	1.50
15CL3	Hall of Famers	1973	1.50
81AL2	All Sports Poster in Full Color		2.00

SPECIAL "STARTER" COLLECTION

Start your sports library with this six-in-one box set . . . "THE BIG 4," "STANLEY CUP," "WORLD SERIES," "GREAT OLYMPIANS," "NBA-ABA PLAYOFF," "GOLF'S BIG 3" . . . Plus bonus all-pro sports large action poster **66AS2** Boxed—set **$4.50**

A $6.50 value, **only $4.50.** Great for Gift-Giving, too!

On any book order over $3.00, ALL SPORTS POSTER FREE! Just mark **81AL2** on your order.

PLEASE ALLOW 4 WEEKS FOR DELIVERY.

12" LONG PLAYING RECORDS — $3.50 EACH

501 **"How To Watch Pro Football" with illustrated text and NFL Rules by Coach Curt Gowdy**

502 **"All Star Tips on How to Play Baseball." One hour of instruction by Superstars.**

FREE! Any two 75¢ books free with an order of $10 or more.

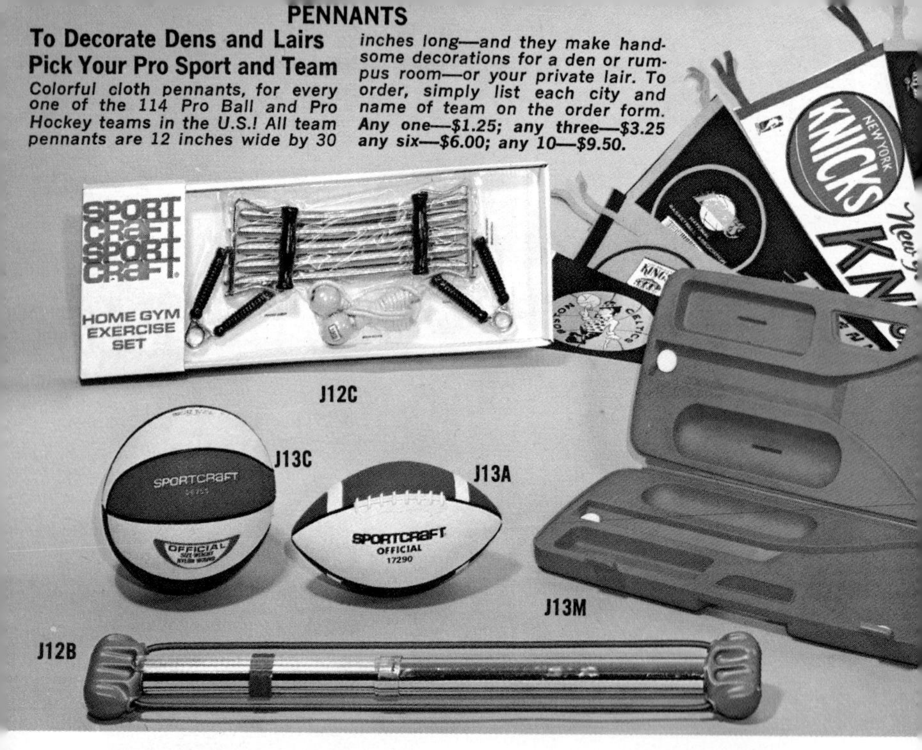

BULLWORKER II. Exercise works. We all know that. But Bullworker isometrics — exercise with a purpose — is four times faster! No other fitness trainer can give you results so quickly and so easily. The secret is isometric contraction — training the muscles of your body to follow precise paths to exert pressure, **briefly,** against controlled resistance.

Briefly is the word! All it takes is seven seconds a day per muscle group — 70 seconds a day of controlled exercise — using just 60% of your natural strength . . . to build more powerful muscles, broader shoulders, trim inches off your waist, make you feel and look stronger and healthier and more vigorous. And there is no sweat.

No elaborate preparations, no monotonous calisthenics, no bulky complex weights or pulleys or bicycle machines. Just you and Bullworker — and 70 seconds a day.

Try Bullworker — for just 14 days — and watch your muscle tone change. More — watch your muscles grow in power — which you can measure with the built in "Power Meter" measuring gauge. Try Bullworker for two weeks, watch your mirror — and if you cannot tell the difference in the way you feel, look, act, simply return the unit and we'll promptly refund your money.

Bullworker is assembled by hand, has a built in compression steel spring which is permanently set and will never slacken. Impossible to break. Chrome plated. Guaranteed for five years. Bullworker is just 34½ inches long, and weighs in at only 3½ pounds — but what it can do for you in 70 seconds a day can be a revelation. The most difficult part of such daily training is the "decision to start." Try it now — you have nothing to lose but your sluggishness and your bulge. **J12B $39.95**

HOME GYM EXERCISE SET. Here is a low cost fitness and body building kit for the sports buff. Five strand chrome plated Chest Expander with colored wood handles. Set also includes a pair of tension Hand Grips with wooden handles, and a durable 8 foot long cotton Jump Rope. **J12C $11.50**

SPORTCRAFT RED, WHITE, AND BLUE RUBBER FOOTBALL . . . with black seams and two white stripes. Official size and weight, with no-slip deep-tread pebbling for better grip and passing control. Self-sealing rubber valve. **J13A $10.25**

Also Spalding genuine brown cowhide football. Off'l size and weight. **J13B $9.50**

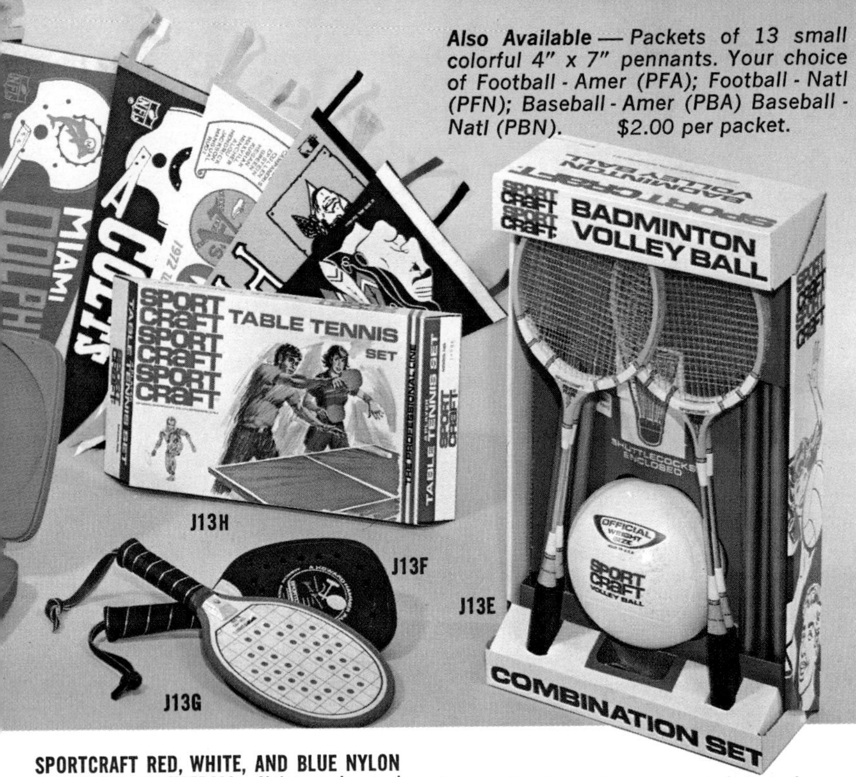

SPORTCRAFT RED, WHITE, AND BLUE NYLON —RUBBER BASKETBALL. Nylon-cord-wound rubber basketball has a rugged scuff-resistant finish, no-slip deep tread pebbling for easier dribbling, passing, shooting, plus self-sealing rubber valve. Official size and weight. **J13C $10.75**

Also Spalding heavy permalite nylon Off'l weight basketball—brown. **J13D $9.50**

BADMINTON — VOLLEY BALL SET . . . sets you up for both badminton and volley ball. You get a set of extra-heavy-gauge steel posts, a 20-foot x 2-foot all-purpose net, 4 deluxe Silver Flash badminton rackets . . . with expert-style steel shaft, leather grip, strung with twisted nylon . . . plus two plastic shuttlecocks. Also one official size lawn volley ball. **J13E $19.95**

Rubber 10 oz. official size molded volley ball with nylon cord winding. **J13K $7.50**

Vinyl 10 oz. official size **J13L $3.50**

TABLE TENNIS SETS . . . Heavy-duty ¾ inch metal extension posts . . . 1 5/6" slip-on metal sleeve net . . . 4 official balls . . . official rules. Choose **J13J**, with four 5-ply piped, rubber-faced paddles . . . with natural cork handles . . . or **J13H**, with four 5-ply soft-style rubber sandwich face paddles with hardwood handles: **J13J $13.50**
J13H $11.50

PADDLE TENNIS PADDLE. 7-ply hardwood paddle with 34 holes drilled in face; bound with heavy rubber for maximum safety. Complete with leather grip wrist strap. **J13F $12.00**

HOWARD HAMMER PADDLE . . . designed by the champion of Paddleball provides sensitive weight distribution and a new hitting surface, plus a contoured handle and grip. Heavily bound. Accurately balanced. 34 holes. Crafted from the finest 5-ply rock maple. **J13G $18.00**

RACQUETTE CASSETTE . . . cradles your racquet (metal or wood), a can of tennis balls, and your headband, sweatband, or other small accessories . . . in 3 fitted compartments. Handsome, lightweight case of durable plastic provides complete protection. Perfect for both travel and storage. 28" long, 11" wide, 4" thick; weighs just 4 lbs. Specify blue . . . white . . . orange . . . yellow . . . black. **J13M $15.75**

BOWMAR; THE DEPENDABLE PERSONAL CALCULATOR: Compact 3"x5"x1"; weighs only 12 oz. You can carry it around in your pocket. Yet does the job of big machines. Eight digit read-out (to 99,999,999) . . . lets you add, subtract, multiply, divide. Even allows chain or mixed multiplication and division using a stored constant. Has floating decimal point and plus or minus sign capability. Comes with rechargeable batteries and charger; operates on batteries or A.C. complete with manufacturer's one-year warranty in zipped vinyl case. At new low price. **J14A $119.95**

J14A

J14B

J14C

J14D

OPTIX. Here's a complete, compact optical and photographic laboratory in a single kit —You get a set of 11 optically correct lenses, a prism, over 114 precision-engineered components . . . including filters, chemicals, and mirrors plus over 250 diagrams — all you need to perform 135 optical experiments and constructions detailed in the 112-page Optix manual. A real scientific eye opener! **J14B $18.75**

ELECTRIX. A masterful electrical lab that takes the mystery out of the fascinating world of electricity . . . Contains every component needed detailed and diagrammed in the 112-page Electrix manual. Simple instructions . . . Build switches . . . work wonders with magnetism . . . build a practical burglar alarm system! Real learning excitement. **J14C $15.75**

LOGIX. Even a 12-year-old can assemble this electronic computer in about two hours, following the detailed illustrated instructions. "Snap-in" assembly requires no soldering. 112 page programming manual has 39 different programs — You play games with the computer, program it, play computerized chess, then build on what you've learned . . . A first rate introduction to computers. **J14D $27.95**

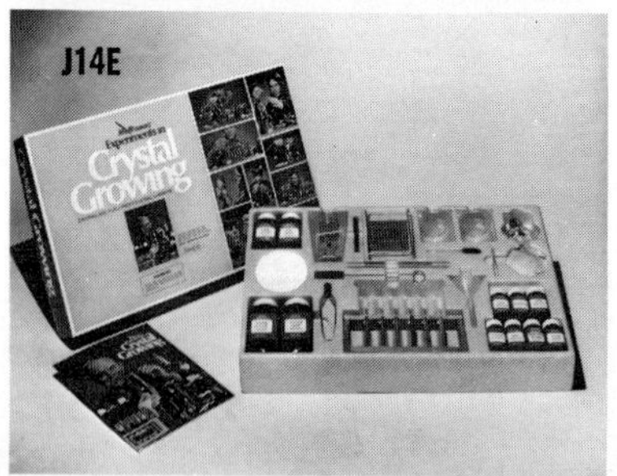

J14E

MR. WIZARD'S EXPERIMENTS IN CRYSTAL GROWING. This unique scientific set lets youngsters grow fascinating, colorful crystals, using the chemicals provided plus such common household products as sugar and salt. Create art objects, sparkling shapes . . . even jewelry. 32-page manual helps young minds. **J14E $22.50**

Other Mr. Wizard Scientific Sets for Bright Young Minds

Ecology Set		**J14F**	**$23.50**
Chemistry		**J14G**	**14.75**
Electronics—(Solid State)	**I**	**J14H**	**11.95**
	II	**J14J**	**19.95**

FREE! Any two 75¢ books free with an order of $10 or more.

REEL LIVE FISHING KITS with famous Martin Reels and Martin Rods. Basic Starter Kit— everything you need to catch fish except the lake. Includes a Model 220 Star Drag Reel, 80 yards of 6 lb. Test monofilament line. Two-piece 5½ ft. solid fiberglass rod, with set of four lures in plastic case, and all within a sturdy nylon carrying case with handle. Be a Huckleberry Finn. **J15K $12.50**

If you are a Pro, choose the **Pro Fisherman Outfit.** No. 700 Star Drag Reel with fast retrieval (15" with each turn of the handle). 100 yards of 8 lb. test monofilament line. Two-piece 6 ft. Flexible Hi-Action tubular fiberglass rod. Four lures in plastic case. Sturdy case with handle. Catch fish like a pro. **J15L $22.95**

A FLASHLIGHT THAT'S READY WHEN YOU NEED IT — the 5 year light . . . with a startling new concept in lighting (developed for government, now offered public for first time). Has proven storage capacity for at least five years! Ten times staying power of ordinary units. No external switches to corrode or break, per NASA specs. Never replace a battery. Never be in the dark again. **J15M $6.95**

TRUE BINOCULARS FOR SPORTS FANS. If you want to see all the action, be sure you have a true prism binocular — don't be fooled by "field glasses" which are imitation binoculars. The ideal sports binocular has 6 to 8 times magnification, is compact, light weight (under 24 oz.) and can be carried easily all day. All complete with cases.

7 x 35. Most popular model. Field of view 367 feet at 1000 yards. Weight 22 oz. **J15E $32.95**

7 x 50. Ideal for spotting. 50mm lens allows greater light gathering; you can see from dawn to dusk. 372 feet at 1000 yards. **J15F $39.95**

8 x 40. High power. Fast center focusing wheel. 351 feet. 23 oz. **J15G $36.95**

8 x 30. Extra power in compact size. Weighs only 18 ozs. 393 feet. **J15H $32.50**

OUTSTANDING GERMAN PEDOMETERS . . . With built-in stride or jogging adjustment. Can be crown set with precision and accuracy. Simplified dial makes reading distances in ¼ miles easy and accurate. Highest quality skilled German craftsmanship. Sturdily built. Can be worn on belt or attached to pocket.

Choose from three styles:

12 mile for better gradation	**J15A**	**$ 8.95**
25 mile for longer hikes	**J15B**	**$ 8.95**
25 mile with deluxe German made compass on back	**J15C**	**$10.95**

NOW — measure your drives. Lower your golf score immediately with pendulum-action GOLF METER. Precise German made instrument tells you how far you've hit the ball in yards — so you know exact distance to the pin. Adjusts to your golfing stride. Clips on belt or pocket. Pocket watch size. Fully guaranteed. **J15D $9.95**

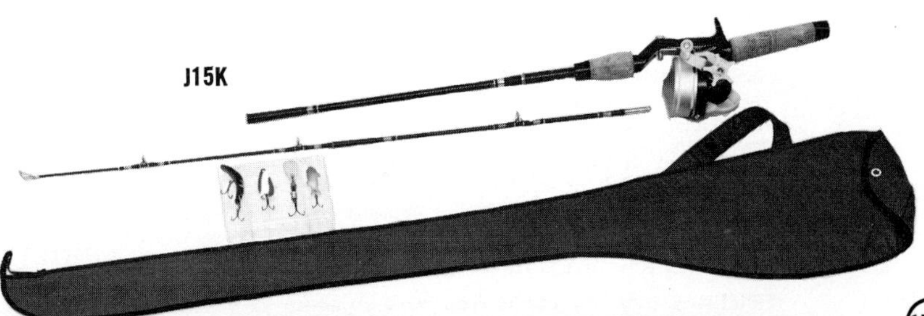

LABYRINTH. Co-ordination is the name c the game! The question is "How far ca you maneuver the shining silver ball throug the maze?" You manipulate two controls t tip the surface just enough to keep the ba moving. Or does the maze trap you? Sma and sleek enough for desk or coffee tabl Big enough challenge for hours of fur competition, and concentration. **J16B $8.9**

LOVE SCULPTURE. You'll love to live wit this beautiful replica of the world-famou "LOVE" sculpture by Robert Indiana. Re produced in heavy polished sculpted meta "LOVE" serenely stands 3⅛" high, 3" wide and 1½" deep. You've never ever seen lovelier 3-dimensional treatment of "LOVE" letter. In its own handsome gi box. **J16A $10.0**

MORE POSTERS FOR YOU!

All 2'x3' in full color. Any one for $2.00

(For complete list of over 90 All-Star Posters, check list of players by team on page 7-G).

771—Moto Cross

766—Ski Jump

747—Pipeline

759—Sky Diving

S3N51—Dick Butkus

7B1—Wilt Chamberlain

7H1—Ed Giacomin

761—"Line up"

780—Globetrotters

FREE! Any two 75¢ books free with an order of $10 or more.

ARNOLD PALMER

A TOUCH OF MAGIC AND AN 'ARMY'

■ He walks down the fairways with the hurrying strut that helped foster the image of the Arnold Palmer charge. A golf glove flaps from his back pocket and a cigarette often dangles from his lips. He doesn't stop until he has reached the spot where his ball lies, unless it's to watch an airplane pass overhead.

"Arnie stops to watch planes fly by, and I find myself doing it too," says Jack Lewis, a young pro who carries a golf glove in his back pocket and holds Palmer up as his idol.

It's difficult to think of Palmer as an idol to the younger golfers on the pro tour. It seems like only yesterday that he burst upon the golf scene with the right combination of talent and charisma and thrust the sport into the floodlights of television, and thus into

the mainstream of American life. There have been better technicians than Palmer—Bobby Jones, Ben Hogan and perhaps even Jack Nicklaus. But Palmer is something special, a golfer with a touch of magic.

Arnie became golf's first millionaire, and yet he remained unchanged by his fortune. Success didn't spoil Palmer and this made his fans—Arnie's Army—appreciate him even more. People root for him to get richer, and he usually does. Despite the fact that he now rarely wins a major tournament or is even a factor in one, Palmer, at 43, makes over $100,000 a year in prize money. And he is still the darling of the galleries. When he gave Nicklaus a run for the money in the 1972 U.S. Open at Pebble Beach, it was in front of the most ambitious television coverage ever accorded a golf event. If anything, Palmer won new legions of followers.

There were personable golfers in the pre-Palmer era, and some have even come into prominence during his reign. But none caught on as Palmer did. He became

Gary Player fires wedge shot at green during Westchester Classic.

synonymous with golf, the sport's best salesman. His popularity helped build interest—and the purses—on the tournament trail. Though he doesn't keep up a running conversation with the galleries as Lee Trevino does, Arnie reaches the spectators through his expressions. It's obvious when he's pleased or displeased with a shot. Fans can see pain, anger, frustration and delight written across his face. Arnold Palmer is no mechanical man.

Palmer made his first impact on the golf world in 1954 when he won the U.S. Amateur championship at the Country Club of Detroit in Grosse Point, Mich. Then 25, Arnie was known as a strongman off the tee who had the potential to become a huge success as a pro. But no one knew just how much of a success Palmer would really be.

Arnie now owns and pilots a jet plane. He has investments and business dealings in real estate, securities and golf equipment. He is one of Madison Avenue's favorite athletes for promotional work. When Palmer endorses a product, it sells. People identify with him—just a common man from Latrobe, Pa., making good. He is Walter Mitty to more than one weekend hacker.

Palmer, however, did not have immediate success when he turned pro. The other golfers weren't exactly in awe of him and he had a lot to prove. In his first year on the tour, he drove a battered old car with a trailer attached behind, one that housed Palmer and his wife Winnie. It was a far cry from the jets that now fly him from one stop to another on the tour.

Arnie was just another youngster and not doing too well at the start. He finished low in the standings and usually won just enough to pay his way to the next tournament. When he turned pro in 1954, he wasn't even allowed the luxury of taking home any prize money.

"It was rough," recalls Arnie. "Under PGA rules, I couldn't take any prize money for six months, so I had to scrape. I tried to play in all the pro-amateur tournaments, prior to the big ones, because you could make a couple of hundred winning those. Of course, the non-PGA tournaments were very important then, too."

After a year of trying, Palmer broke through in 1955 when he won the Canadian Open and earned $7,958.00 on the tour. Purses weren't as big in those days and his winnings enabled Arnie to rank 32nd among the money leaders. More important, he was able to begin paying back the debts he had accumulated the year before. By the end of 1957, the young strongman had raised his money winnings to the $30,000 level and had won several tournaments, including the San Diego Open, the Houston Open and the Eastern Open.

The golf world was beginning to sit up and take notice. In 1958, Arnie vaulted to the top of the money-winning list as he won the Masters, his first major tournament, and also took down first place in the St. Petersburg Open and the Pepsi Championship. Arnie won $42,607, enough to lead all the pros. Since then he has won the Masters three more times, the British Open twice and the U.S. Open once (in 1960). He has lost three playoffs for the U.S. Open title, which has left him frustrated, but not as much as his failure to win the PGA tournament, the fourth leg of the Grand Slam.

The tournament victory that made the biggest impression on the golfing public was the 1960 Masters. It was the occasion of Arnie's second Masters win and his first dramatic charge before millions of viewers. At the 17th hole of the final round, Palmer needed a birdie to tie the leader, Ken Venturi, who was in the clubhouse and seemingly safe with a final total of 283.

Those on the tour were about to learn, however, that no lead was safe as long as Palmer and his fans were still out on the course. The thunder of Arnie's Army can be heard all over the course. The roar signifies only one thing: Palmer has begun his charge. It has unnerved a few rivals and made others feel uncomfortable. It can be disastrous for a golfer who is playing as Palmer's partner.

The roar was never louder than that day in 1960 when Palmer left himself 25 feet short of the birdie he needed on the 17th hole at Augusta. He stroked the ball boldly and then watched as it began the dramatic roll to the cup. It lingered at the tip and dropped in. The "Army" exploded in sound.

A par on the 18th would give Palmer a tie and force a playoff the following day. But Arnie rarely plays for a tie; nor did he in his early days on the tour. Every shot is stroked to go in the cup, from his powerful drives to the pitch shots from off the green to those bold, gambling putts.

On the 18th, Palmer whispered to his caddy: "No tie. Let's go for the bird." He played two fantastic

Arnold Palmer's personality always shows through on the golf course.

shots, the second of which hit the cup and left him five feet short of outright victory. He studied the putt ("It was the most nervous moment in my career.") and he stroked it into the cup. Arnie had won the Masters. Later, he spoke of the goals he had set for himself. "I want to win the Grand Slam . . . I think it would be a greater achievement than the Grand Slam scored by Bobby Jones in 1930."

It was more of a dream than a goal for Palmer. He won the U.S. Open in 1960 but has never been able to come close to the Grand Slam. For a while, in 1963, there were even rumors he was washed up. They said he had made too much money and no longer cared. "I heard those rumors and I didn't like them. I wanted to show people they weren't true."

Palmer left the tour temporarily and sharpened his game. He came back to win the 1964 Masters and go over the $100,000 mark in prize winnings again. Not that his avid followers had ever doubted him. It's just that people had come to expect perfection, and Arnie was not a perfectionist.

"When things get to be too much, when they get to be tough," Arnie has said, "I like to pick up and leave the tour for a while. I go home to Latrobe and fool around with caddies, and I knock around some clubs in the shop and I play a little golf with the local guys. It relaxes me."

Even today, as once again the rumors persist that Arnie is no longer capable of fashioning the dramatic charges of a decade ago, he is still a player to be reckoned with. Perhaps Palmer has lost part of the touch that made him the best, but fellow pros still cringe with anticipation when he shows up for a tournament. At 43, he is still capable of winning a major tournament, even though he may have lost some of the old Palmer magic.

Palmer today is the same man who won that first memorable Masters victory in 1958. "I like to get away, to walk around in old shoes and wrinkled slacks and a sweater," he smiles. "I think all the success came so fast for me that I never learned to feel comfortable with it. I'm still a plain country guy, and I like the plain things.

"Dinner with Winnie, playing friendly golf, working in the pro shop, tinkering with clubs . . . that's where it's at for me. That's the real life. Those are the important things. The rest is great; golf gave it to me, but I still like to think I'm a regular guy who just happened to play a couple of good rounds of golf."

A regular guy, perhaps, but Arnold Palmer just didn't happen to play a couple of good rounds of golf. His talent is rare, and he has made the most of it. He has given much to golf and many exciting memories to the members of "Arnie's Army."

It would be difficult to mention the Palmer years without including Gary Player. He shadowed Palmer on the tour, always ready to pounce on the first prize if Arnie didn't. Later, Palmer and

Palmer, wearing glasses these days, follows flight of ball to the green.

Player were joined by Jack Nicklaus, and the 1960s belonged to the three of them.

As opposed to an extrovert such as Palmer, Gary Player is a quiet man who goes about his business as if he hoped no one would notice him. As opposed to Palmer's size and great strength, Player is only five-foot-eight and weighs 160 pounds. He's not a long hitter but he's an accurate hitter. He is also a physical fitness buff who is always in excellent condition.

Gary is from Johannesburg, South Africa, and during his early years on the American tour, he spent precious little time at home. He is a devoted family man and it disturbed him. But Player had made up his mind to earn his fortune in golf and then return home to enjoy it with his family. In recent years, he has spent less time in the United States and, in 1972, he was only a part-time player on the tour. Yet, he still earned over $100,000 and won the prestigious Professional Golf Association (PGA) championship for the second time.

Player has also won the Masters (1961), the U.S. Open (1965) and twice has won the British Open (1959 and 1968). He is among the top six money-winners of all time and now, at 36, he has reached a point where he could give up competitive golf and retire as a wealthy young man.

But it is difficult to envision the tour without Gary. Though quiet, he is far from a colorless person. The galleries took to the small South African who dressed in the familiar black shirt and slacks, with a white cap. This outfit became Player's trademark, as much as the make-up of his stylish swing.

"A golfer's scores always seem to go up as he ages," says Player. "But I see no reason for this to happen. Golf is a game of fractions and inches, and your reflexes must be kept razor-sharp. When a man begins to age, his reflexes start slowing down almost imperceptibly. But if you work hard at maintaining them, you can continue to play top golf."

Sometimes the pressures on Player have been rough. The government of South Africa practices a policy of apartheid. Many thought Gary would receive adverse publicity in the U.S. as a representative of that government. Yet, he has managed to handle this ticklish situation with the same unflappable style that is characteristic of his play on the golf course.

Player made a million friends after he won the U.S. Open in 1965 at Bellerive in St. Louis and donated the prize money of $30,000 to the Caddies' Scholarship Fund. "Golf in the United States has been good to me," he said, "and I should like to do something good for American golf in return."

Gary's first victory on the American tour came in 1958 when he won the Kentucky Derby Open. He had played the tour the year before with only moderate success, winning $3,286. In 1958,

Billy Casper, one of golf's "old guard," won the Open in 1959 and 1965.

DEMING
MENOMINEE, MICH.
DOBIE

however, he began to establish himself as a factor in every tournament. And in the ensuing years he gradually earned more and more until 1969, when he went over the $100,000 barrier, winning $123,897. He attributes his success to physical fitness.

"For a man like me, fitness is the whole story. I can't hit as long as the big men but I stay in shape and play each shot as if the entire tournament is riding on it."

The victory in the U.S. Open was probably Player's greatest triumph. The Bellerive course, built for the talents of the power hitters such as Palmer and Nicklaus, played long. But after the final round, Player found himself deadlocked with Australian Ken Nagle. Gary had shot steady rounds of 70-70-71-71–282. Nagle was more erratic, but a final round of 69 had enabled him to forge a tie. On the following day, Player shot another workmanlike round of 71, while Nagle registered a 74, and in the process, twice hit fans in the gallery.

Player did not allow the playoff pressure to change his game. "I can't change my game to fit the situation," he said. "If I tried to do that, I wouldn't win anything. I'm not the greatest golfer in the world, and I can't afford to take any chances. I guess I'm a conservative."

Conservative in play and conservative in dress, Player still reigns as a favorite of the galleries. "I wear black because it is the plainest color I know," he says. "I don't like to be flashy or showy. My game is golf, not entertainment, and I dress to be comfortable, mentally as well as physically." It's worked for Gary Player and this is all that's really important.

Plain? Never! Showy? Just about every time he walks on the course. At one extreme there is Gary Player. At the other, watch out, here comes SuperMex. Here comes Lee Trevino, his mouth flapping before, during and after almost every shot. If the gallery is there strictly to appreciate a man's talents on the golf course, as Player insists, Trevino views it as a supper club audience. He's the comedian and they respond to his quips as much as they do to his magnificent ability with a golf club.

There probably has never been a golfer like Lee Trevino, or at least never one as successful for the amount of clowning he does. He grew up a poor Mexican-American, and to this day he is like a ghetto kid who wakes up one morning to find a million dollar check under a torn and featherless pillow. Lee Trevino is having fun getting rich and he isn't about to let the staid world of professional golf stop him from enjoying the experience.

Lee is an example to the poor, to the kids roaming the streets. Trevino is one of them, a kid who could have turned out bad but didn't. Not all poor youngsters can play golf as well as Trevino, but some may be able to do it in other sports. Some may do it through education. Whatever way

Bruce Crampton wins a lot of money on U.S. tour—but doesn't smile much.

they choose, Trevino proved it can be done if a person puts his mind to it.

The happy little Mexican burst upon the golf scene in 1968, when he won the U.S. Open at Rochester. He also captured the Hawaiian Open that year and finished with earnings of $132,127. He went over the $100,000 mark in 1969 and again in 1970. In 1971, Lee won the U.S., British and Canadian Opens, and in 1972 he took home over $200,000. Trevino made himself a household word. Soon the man who was born in a shack was doing television commercials for expensive cars. He became a favorite of Madison Avenue and it gave him an opportunity to do what he does only second best to playing golf. Introduce Lee Trevino and sit back and enjoy the show.

Trevino was born out of wedlock on Dec. 1, 1939. He was raised by his grandfather, Joe Trevino, who was originally from Monterrey, and by his mother, Juanita. They lived in an old shack on the outskirts of Dallas and Joe Trevino earned his living as a gravedigger.

"He was also the only man I ever knew who could sit in a bar from nine in the morning to nine at night, then get up and drive away," Lee says with a smile.

It was not the best example to set for grandson Lee, who used to wait in the fields near a golf course during the day and hunt for balls. He occasionally used an old five iron to occupy his time playing with the balls he found.

"It was a lonely life," Trevino reflects. "I was never around anybody. I was all by myself, no one to talk to. I'd just go hunt rabbits and fish."

Lee, who quit school in the eighth grade, never had the benefit of a balanced diet. He had to find a job so his family, which included two sisters, could eat. "Starches are cheap and Mexicans are usually overweight because they eat starches," he says. "I never knew what steak was. The closest we ever came to real meat was Texas hash and baloney. We drank Kool-Aid."

Trevino worked around golf courses, where he had an opportunity to improve his game. But he was lazy and he had little initiative. Finally, he quit to join the Marines, where he spent time in the Far East.

"I was messed up and lost," he says today. "I wasn't settled down. I didn't know what I wanted to do. Never had any dates. But in the Marines, there were guys my own age and we had a ball. It was like camping out."

Lee reenlisted for two years and was assigned to Special Services. He was able to practice his golf a good deal of the time and his game improved. "Maybe it was the best time of my life," he says. "I think I learned my sense of humor in the Marines, laughing and raising hell. And of course, there was golf. If I hadn't joined, I know I'd be in prison today." He left the Marines in 1960 and there was no chance Lee Trevino was going to prison. He had one thing

Sam Snead, a star from another golfing era, is still challenging the kids.

on his mind and that was golf. Professional golf. Hardy Greenwood, a 56-year-old driving range operator, hired Lee and then spent most of his time becoming a second father to him. He encouraged Trevino to make golf a living.

"We always like to say we raised Lee," Hardy states. "We take the credit. He had the great natural swing even back then. He was good at everything. He picked up balls faster than anyone. He mowed the greens, washed balls, cleaned the range, ran the shop. I could go out of town and Lee would take better care of the place than I did. I told him the last time he was here, 'You sure did grow up to be the smartest Mex I ever saw.' "

Trevino got up early every morning to play golf before work, and soon he was the best in the area. He also displayed the ability to think; he was more than just a strong hitter who couldn't make evaluations and decisions on the course.

"There are a lot of fine strikers of the ball," Jack Nicklaus says. "Trevino is a fine striker and a fine thinker. He knows what he's doing all the time. Where to hit. What to hit. And why to hit it."

Trevino was able to evaluate the course in each tournament and plan how many strokes it should take him to play each hole. "I think about what I should make on every hole in every tournament. For instance, if I've got a par-3, 220-yard hole, I'll hope to play the thing in one over par for four rounds. I won't go for the pin, just the green, and almost never gamble."

Despite his strength and calculating mind, Trevino does have weaknesses. However, contrary to popular opinion, it's not true his game would improve if he were to do less talking on the course.

"Weaknesses? There are a lot of them," he admits. "I'm a terrible fairway bunker player and I used to be the world's worst putter. But playing on good greens has helped me there. I also used to be a very bad long iron player. Up until two years ago, I couldn't hit a two or three iron for nothing. But I practiced."

If there is anything Trevino loves, it's to go head-to-head with another golfer. And when that golfer is Nicklaus, it seems to bring out the best in the happy Mex.

Though Nicklaus rarely com-

Ken Venturi's career went into decline after dramatic 1964 U.S. Open win.

plains, it is obvious that the outgoing nature of Trevino disturbs his concentration on the course. Jack has been known to stand over a putt longer than any golfer on the tour. It reaches a point where some touring pros complain about his slow play. But Trevino doesn't waste much time. And the way he keeps talking—to galleries, caddies and fellow golfers—must make Nicklaus wonder how Lee keeps any semblance of concentration.

"On the greens, I'll tell my caddie: 'That thing broke a ton, Neil,' when I actually pulled the putt. The other guy, he might hit his putt wrong now. Course, I only did this sort of thing before I got to the tour," Trevino says, without too much conviction.

When Trevino lined up at the first tee of his playoff with Nicklaus for the 1971 U.S. Open title at Merion, he took a rubber snake from his bag and set it down on the tee. Some were flabbergasted, but this time Nicklaus welcomed the prank. "I thought it would relieve the tension," says Lee." It relaxed me."

Trevino eventually discarded the snake, but has not cut down on the amount of talking he does. "Some acts are a facade, a fake," a fellow pro observes. "Lee is as sincere as he can be. He fools around and then he hits the ball. But for the twenty seconds it takes to select the club and make the shot, he's as much a Hogan—a concentrator—as anybody ever was."

A perfect entertainer, Trevino has sometimes run into difficulties because of his outspoken ways. Until 1972, he had never played in the Masters, claiming the Augusta course did not fit his style. Finally he relented—but did not play well. In the summer of 1970, he failed to show at the first tee for the opening round of the Westchester Classic, which offers a first prize of $50,000. He was disqualified despite his plea that he had overslept. He has not been the model of consistency, for all his winnings. Twice he's had to leave the tour—once for an appendix operation, and again because he caught pneumonia.

Still, Trevino maintains his popularity and following. "I could be a comedian," he chuckles. "I know when to raise my voice and when not to. I tell jokes on the course, but it's not too often Mexes get inside the ropes. You think I'm good in tournaments? Oh, boy. Come to a clinic. You get 18 holes of golf plus a comedy act. But I'm worth it."

Although Lee is an endless talker, he reveals little of his real inner feelings. "He's a hard man to get close to," a fellow golfer says. "He has a few friends out there, but even they don't know him too well. I've never had a serious conversation with him. Every time we'd start, he'd go into that meaningless machine-gun yak of his. And then he'd have to leave and go someplace. It's like he's afraid to shut up so we can find out what he's really like."

On the golf course, there are no mysteries about Trevino. He has replaced Arnold Palmer and Gary Player as the biggest threat to any title Nicklaus has set his sights on. In 1971, it was the three Open titles which earned Trevino the distinction of Athlete of the Year. Then, in 1972, with his golf game sub-par because of his bout with pneumonia, Trevino ended Nicklaus' dream of the Grand Slam by winning the British Open for the second straight year.

And just as Gary Player was generous, so is Trevino. He has donated $10,000 to the family of his former roommate, Ted Makalena; $2,000 for a caddie scholarship fund; $5,000 to the St. Jude Hospital in Memphis; $4,800 to an orphanage in the British Isles, and other donations for the Christmas and Easter Seal programs and Boys Clubs. He remembers his humble beginnings and tries to share his success with others.

His wife and two of his three children live in El Paso. Lee calls the Southwest his home and is planning a new home and golf course on the New Mexico border. While he will rarely turn down an opportunity to party, his roots are still in the hot sun and dust, where he grew up.

At one time, in 1970, success seemed to be getting to Trevino. He kept late hours, drank more than was his habit and was running into business problems. His mother was dying of cancer and there were rumors that his marriage was breaking up. His golf game suffered. Soon his wife Claudia made several stops on the tour with Lee, and he cut short the night life.

"I was depressed when I remembered my mother being so ill

In his prime, Ben Hogan was the most dominant golfer on the pro tour.

(she has since died)," he said. "But I stopped that quick. I visited a lot of hospitals with crippled kids and burned up people in them. Men with car payments and kids to put through college should visit a hospital whenever they start feeling sorry for themselves."

A very sensitive man, with an outgoing personality and a desire to please, Lee Trevino, in some ways, is the most complex player on the tour. One thing is certain: Trevino now ranks behind only Nicklaus as the most dominant golfer of the time. And there are those who would argue that he should be first.

Perhaps the biggest victory in Bill Casper's career will be remembered more as the tournament Arnold Palmer lost rather than the tournament that Casper won. It was the 1965 U.S. Open when Palmer lost seven strokes on the final round with only nine holes to play. Casper made up the deficit to tie for the championship at the Lake Course Olympic Country Club in San Francisco, and then defeated Palmer in a playoff the next day.

Of course, this wasn't the first tournament ever won by the man who ranks third on the all-time money winning list behind Palmer and Nicklaus. Casper took his first U.S. Open in 1959 and has also won the Bob Hope Classic, the Western Open, the Los Angeles and Hartford Opens, and the Doral Open. In all, he has won 41 tournaments. Most of the time, however, the 41-year-old Casper has taken a back seat to golf's Big Three of Palmer, Player and Nicklaus.

"Those other men were the top golfers and it was only right for them to receive top billing," Casper says modestly.

Casper, though, has more than held up his own against the Big Three. Since 1955 he has been a model of consistency on the tour—and a deadly putter. Billy accomplished a great deal despite a highly allergic condition which required him to stay on a special diet that often sapped his strength. It's not unusual to find Casper eating bear steak, carrot and beet juice and sesame bread.

Billy still hadn't received much recognition until he staged that dramatic comeback against Palmer in the U.S. Open. "It seemed everytime I looked around, Casper was another stroke closer," Palmer said. "I was nervous and finally I began to wonder."

"I was just playing to hold on to second place that day," Casper recalls. "First place never crossed my mind until the fifteenth hole." After Casper had won the playoff, he asked: "Is it real? It's like a dream. It's something I've been hoping and praying for. It's very rewarding." Palmer said nothing.

"My outlook on golf," Casper states, "is one of thankfulness. Golf has meant more to me than I ever imagined it would. It has provided my family with security and a good life, and I am proud to be playing with such people as you find on the tour. There are only four interests that occupy me. They are religion (he's a devout Mormon), family, golf and fishing, in that order."

The way Casper plays, though, most pros would say golf was his first priority, his major interest.

Before the Big Three emerged as a dominating force and after the era of Bobby Jones and the now-legendary Grand Slam, golf was ruled by the Big Two of Ben Hogan and Sam Snead. Hogan was regarded as a perfectionist in the mold of Jones and Nicklaus, and many still consider him the finest golfer who ever lived.

It almost ended abruptly for Bantam Ben in February of 1949, when his car went out of control on a Texas highway near the small town of Van Horn and smashed into an oncoming bus. That Ben Hogan lived was a miracle. That he lived to play golf again was more than a miracle.

Before the accident Hogan had already established himself as one of the finest shotmakers in the history of the game. He won the U.S. Open in 1948, the PGA in 1946 and 1948, was runnerup in the 1946 Masters and was a member of the 1947 Ryder Cup team. Then came the tragic accident.

Doctors and police at the scene thought he was dead, but his wife Valerie heard a barely audible groan. And some four hours after the crash, Ben Hogan was removed to Hotel Dieu Hospital in El Paso. He had suffered a broken collarbone, a double fracture of the pelvis, a fractured left ankle, smashed ribs and other internal injuries. It was two days before doctors dared move him and even when he survived the early crises, doctors doubted he would live. "There is legitimate reason to fear that Ben Hogan will never walk again," a doctor said. "He is lucky simply to be alive."

Ben fought back, however, and the injuries began to heal. If anyone had the courage and determination to make it all the way back, it was Hogan. Just as he started winning the battle, another setback occurred when blood clots began to develop in his legs. The doctors at the hospital were not qualified to perform the surgery to drain the major artery and poor weather made it almost impossible for Hogan to be moved. He became delirious and finally his brother, Royal, the commanding officer of the Briggs Air Force Base in El Paso, had Hogan flown to El Paso.

The operation was performed but circulation in Hogan's left leg was reduced to the minimum. It was feared he wouldn't be able to walk. Even if he did, it was feared he would never play golf. But 12 days later, Hogan headed for Fort Worth and began the strenuous program to regain the strength in his leg.

In January of 1950, less than a year after the accident, Ben Hogan entered the Los Angeles Open. He shot rounds of 73-69-69-69–280 and held the lead as he limped wearily to the clubhouse. But Snead shot a final round of 66 to tie Hogan and force a playoff. The exhausted Hogan could not handle the task. He shot a 76 and Snead won. But Ben Hogan proved he could come back.

The following year, Ben won the U.S. Open and the Masters. Then came 1953, the best year of all for Hogan. He won the Masters, U.S. and British Open—three-out-of-four in the Grand Slam. It was his first attempt at the British Open and he won it easily at Carnoustie, despite a week-long rain which made the course heavy. He was given a ticker-tape parade down Broadway in New York and was presented with the key to the city.

Art Wall, Jr., won the 1959 Masters title using the baseball grip.

"It makes you want to cry," he said. "I owe it to God and to my wife Valerie."

The triumph in the British Open made Hogan famous all over the world. All the greats before him had to win the Open to gain recognition in Europe, and Hogan wasn't any different. "That man was the only golfer I was truly afraid of," said Lloyd Mangrum. It was a feeling shared by many of the game's best players.

Hogan remained a strong competitor through the 1960s, though it became apparent that lingering after-effects of the accident and advancing age would probably keep him from winning any major tournaments. He pulled out of the 1970 Westchester Classic because he was slated to tee off at 7 AM. "I don't know how to play golf at that time of the morning," he said.

Ben's major disappointment was not winning the U.S. Open for a fifth time. His last serious bid came in 1960 when he lost to Arnold Palmer in Denver. But Hogan didn't have to win another tournament to solidify his place in golf history. Merely being able to walk back on the course was a victory of overwhelming proportions.

When Hogan lost that playoff to Snead in the Los Angeles Open in 1950, famed sportswriter Grantland Rice wrote: "He lost to Snead because his legs just weren't strong enough to carry his heart."

His swing is as smooth as any there ever was and some contend that Slammin' Sammy Snead may have the best natural swing of any golfer. He once shot an 86 playing lefthanded and Snead is a righty. In 1945, he toured a course playing with just one hand and shot rounds of 83-82-81. Snead is a natural, a man who can still play a competitive round of golf against the youngsters on the tour. When the seniors tournaments are held, he usually emerges the winner.

And the main reason is his great swing, a thing that borders on perfection. "Ah've tried to keep it simple as possible," he says in his lazy southern drawl. "Ah git those periods, though, when my backswing gits out o' wack."

But not too often. He has won

Two of golf's most colorful figures, Gene Sarazen (left) and Jimmy Demaret.

the PGA and Masters three times and the British Open once. The U.S. Open has eluded him, however, and though it would seem he has passed the point of winning it, Snead still enters each year to give it a try. He has won over 100 pro tournaments, more than any other golfer in history. Many of these triumphs have come in his battles with Hogan.

At 60, Sam Snead manages to stir interest in one or two tournaments every year; he usually comes in with at least one round under 70. But today Snead is more of a golfing legend than a tournament threat.

When the era of Hogan and Snead passed and emergence of Palmer, Player and Nicklaus as superior golfers had become reality, several other players joined Billy Casper in the fight to "steal" a tournament or two away from the Big Three. Often it must have felt like being the runt of the litter for men such as George Archer, Frank Beard, Dave Hill and Tommy Aaron. Not that they starved, exactly. But often all they collected were the leftovers, the less prestigious tournaments that the Big Three would bypass.

Archer is one of the tallest players on the tour at six-foot-six. He won the Masters in 1969—and the famous green blazer didn't fit. He's won the Bing Crosby, the Lucky International and earned over $100,000 for several years. Not bad for leftovers.

Tommy Aaron became known as one of the more successful players on the tour, winning over $100,000 without ever finishing first in any tournament. In 1970 he broke a 10-year dry spell and won the Atlanta Classic. Aaron is always among the leaders and contenders in every tournament he enters. He proved that second place wasn't all that bad.

Frank Beard started his pro career in 1962, but struggled for five years before he hit it rich in 1967. He won the American Classic, the Westchester Classic and New Orleans Open, taking home over $100,000 in prize money. Despite a slump in recent years, Beard remains one of the better players on the tour. He even wrote a book about life as a professional golfer, a diary which included interesting accounts of the trials of his fellow golfers.

At 37, Dave Hill is one of the more outspoken members of the tour who has been fined on occasion for his complaints about golf courses. He called the Chaska, Minnesota, course, site of the 1970 U.S. Open, "a cow pasture." He may lack tact, but Hill has done well on the tour. His best year was 1969, when he won more than $156,000.

Australian Bruce Crampton has been one of the more successful foreign players on the tour, though he is basically a colorless and unemotional man who fails to excite the galleries. He has consistently finished among the leaders in prize money and, in 1970, he won the Westchester Classic.

Though successful in the past, the Old Guard is being challenged by a new breed of young golfer straight from the PGA schools and college campuses. The days of the Big Three would seem to be at an end. ■

EX-'RABBITS' THREATENING PRO GOLF ESTABLISHMENT

■ Their names would usually appear only in the results of the first or second round of a major tournament, and then disappear like a golf ball sinking into the rough. The third and fourth rounds traditionally belonged to the veterans of the pro tour, the game's superstars, the players who knew how to survive the collar-tightening pressure of a $25,000 payday. But if the kids lacked the skills of Nicklaus and Palmer, they most certainly weren't short on persistence. The following week they'd be back again, swinging from the heels off the tee, setting a red-hot pace out of the gate.

The tour veterans and members of the press called them "the rabbits."

Well, "the rabbits" are thriving nowadays, no longer the front-runners who fold when the big money is on the line. And like rabbits, they seem to be multiplying at a rate that makes no tournament secure for an established pro. When Jack Nicklaus isn't worrying about Arnold Palmer, Gary Player, Lee Trevino or Bruce Crampton, he has to contend with the likes of Grier Jones, Tom Weiskopf, Jerry Heard, Johnny Miller, Lanny Wadkins, Jim Jamieson and others among the seemingly unending succession of young stars who now find themselves in contention for golf's big money, week after week.

Every era had its whiz kids, its bright hopes for the future. But never have they been in as great a number as in the early 1970s. While Nicklaus, Trevino, Palmer and other established pros can still be found at the top of the money-winning lists, there is room enough for Grier Jones, Heard,

Tom Weiskopf symbolizes new young stars who are bidding for golf fame.

OPF

Weiskopf, Wadkins, Jamieson and Miller to earn over $100,000 in a single year.

The number of tournaments has increased and the payoffs are larger. Golf has become almost as strong an attraction for the young athlete as any of the other major sports. For those who show better-than-average ability, there is the opportunity to earn as much, if not more, than a football or baseball player, without having to do much more than dress casually in a knit shirt and slacks and walk 18 holes of golf for four days.

Of course, it isn't that easy for everyone. Unlike the other major sports, golf does not guarantee an income and a young pro or a veteran having a poor year can literally go hungry. There are also dozens of young players who are struggling to make the tour. The ones who do make it don't always win despite the growing success of "the rabbits." For every Miller or Wadkins, there is a Bunky Henry, a player of great promise who struggled home in 1972 with earnings just over $20,000, hardly sufficient to pay his tour expenses. The influx of young talent in golf shouldn't surprise anyone. Athletes in the other professional sports are bigger, stronger and faster than in previous generations. While no one has to race from tee to green, size has helped the college-bred kids accomplish in tow shots what some of the smaller players need three to accomplish. Weiskopf, for instance, is a 6-3 native of Ohio whose distance off the tee has often been compared with that of Nicklaus. At 29, he is the old man of the young set, a holdover from the mid-1960s when an earlier group of young players made their presence felt on the tour.

"I can't hit with Tom," Nicklaus says, paying Weiskopf the highest of compliments. At the Thunderbird Tournament in Westchester in 1965. Weiskopf, then 23, walked up to the 10th hole, a 295-yard straightaway, and promptly hit his first shot over the green.

"Oh, I hit some of them long," he says, "but most of them are crooked."

Weiskopf emerged as the first threat to the Nicklaus—Palmer—Player dynasty, but found it took more than just strength to succeed in golf. He attended Ohio State for two years and made his first splash by winning the Western Amateur in 1963. When he turned pro he became one of those youngsters who would start strong each week and then fade.

"I needed work on my short game." he recalls. "I guess all newcomers do. But then, even the guys who have been here a long time have to keep working on theirs, too."

Sensing Tom's ability, both Palmer and Nicklaus, the latter a fellow alumnus of Ohio State, helped the young star, knowing full well he might one day threaten their reign. Palmer fashioned a putter for him from an old head Weiskopf had found, and Nicklaus changed his grip when both were in college. Nick-

Weiskopf jumps for joy after playoff win in 1971 Kemper Open.

laus also allowed Weiskopf to follow him around and carry his clubs during a number of tournaments in Ohio, so Tom could gain experience.

"He's one of the brighter prospects," Palmer said at the time. "He's got a pretty good swing and he's a pretty good putter. He's got all the shots. These days you need the long ball. The longer and straighter you hit it, the better you're going to be. He's got the long ball, some spirit—which is good—and I believe he has the desire. He's going to have to work at it, though. It's not going to come easy." Weiskopf benefited from the fact that his parents play golf. "Both are pretty good amateurs," he says. "My mother won the Ohio Women's Amateur eight years in a row and my father won a lot of tournaments, too. They still hold the world record of 65 in an amateur Scotch foursome. They could have played the tour if they had the opportunities I had."

Most pros agree that Lanny Wadkins has a great future on pro tour.

Weiskopf received a golf scholarship to Ohio State but quit after two years and just "joked around" a Columbus course in 1963 and 1964. He turned pro late in 1964 and got his player's card early the next year.

But even for a young pro with a wealth of ability, success rarely comes overnight. And that seems to be the case for the youngsters of every era. There are going to be days when they must shoot 67 or 68 merely to qualify for a tournament. Then, it's a struggle just making the cut. Often, if a player succeeds at attaining that modest goal, he is satisfied. The victories come later.

Two years after Weiskopf turned pro, he was still struggling and was not among the leading money winners. Up until the end of 1966, his best effort had been in the Greater Greensboro Open where he tied Doug Sanders for first and then lost in a playoff.

"He can't do anything but get better," veteran Tommy Bolt said at the time. "He'll improve as long as he doesn't try to be the longest hitter in the world."

"I don't care if I'm long as long as I'm straight," Weiskopf said.

But the wisecracks were few and far between as the young Ohio pro continued to find difficulty on the tour despite all the praise offered by the veterans. Sometimes it creates more pressure. If Weiskopf's goals were modest, then the ones set for him by Nicklaus and Palmer were not. He had to live up to the billing they gave him and that proved to be almost impossible.

In 1971 Tom was still young enough at 28, but he was becoming lost in the crowd of new faces, many who resembled him when he first started. No longer could one "rabbit" be singled out for praise. There were a dozen or so with extraordinary ability, and Weiskopf began to look like a graying cotton tail by comparison.

The drought ended for Weiskopf in the middle of June when he won the $150,000 Kemper Open in a four-way playoff. It was his first tournament victory in three years and it was well appreciated, even if it came the hard way.

"It's like shooting craps," Weiskopf said. "If you've got more than one player in a playoff, then sudden death isn't really a major test. A lot of luck enters into it. If you're playing head-to-head, it may be fairer. I don't really like it. I'd only played in two before, and lost in both of them."

All four had finished the regulation 72 holes in 277, but Weiskopf began the day six strokes behind Dale Douglass in what appeared to be another fruitless search for victory. "I didn't think I had a chance to win until I came to 18, and I still thought I was playing for second," he said.

Weiskopf's victory that year raised his earnings at the time to $60,000, and he began to look like the super-star everyone thought had blossomed in 1968 when he won two tournaments.

"After I won those two, I thought I could win them all every time I went out. I started pressing—pressing to shoot a 68 or 69 every round. And I went into a slump. But then in 1969 I did pretty well. I didn't win a tournament, but I had the low stroke average on the tour and I won almost $100,000. And I didn't even play after Labor Day. I took four months off and went hunting."

Bob Murphy earned $105,595 as a rookie on pro tour in 1968.

Weiskopf learned, however, that competition on the tour does not allow any golfer the luxury of relaxing. "I think my game suffered because of it," he said. "But I think it's coming back. For a while, I was beginning to wonder if I was ever going to win another tournament."

By 1972, Weiskopf had made it all the way back. His prize earnings went over $130,000 and he began to finally establish himself on the tour as a threat in every tournament. If he had reached this stage three years earlier, pro golf would have heralded the arrival of the "New Nicklaus." But now Weiskopf must be content to share the limelight with the younger "rabbits."

Of all the young players, none has emerged with more sparkle, shine and ability than Lanny Wadkins, a tour rookie who attended Wake Forest on an Arnold Palmer Golf Scholarship, then beat Arnie by one stroke in the Sahara Invitational in 1972. It was his first victory—but no one believes it will be his last.

Jerry Heard collected over $127,000 in 1972—and is still improving!

More suprisingly, Wadkins' first year netted him $116,000 in prize money—thanks to second place finishes in the Bob Hope and Phoenix Open tournaments, in addition to his one victory. Of course, the results were surprising only to those who didn't believe Wadkins when he claimed he wouldn't be satisfied with anything less than $100,000. "Cocky"—that's how people described him then.

"It's funny about goals. It's hard to sit down and formulate them." Wadkins says. "But once you begin playing, they eventually present themselves. Like last summer, sometime in July, I had already won around $60,000 and I realized I could break Bob Murphy's rookie money record of $105,595 (in 1968). That gave me something to shoot for. So, coming into the Sahara when I had to win to break that record, I got it."

Wadkins' success story started as all golfers' do, even though the moon-faced 23-year-old reached his goal a lot earlier than most. He was a successful amateur, but still was in debt when he started playing on the tour. He went out on his own, without sponsors, and made good. He always had the ability to talk himself a good game; Lanny proved he could play one, too.

"Lanny is the boldest player I've ever seen, probably a lot like

Palmer used to be," observes Johnny Miller, another successful youngster. "People say he's cocky, but he has reason to be. He hits more good shots than most people."

From his peers to veteran pros to caddies, everyone raves about Wadkins. He brings Palmer's facial expressions to the course as he grimaces over a missed putt or breaks out in a smile when he puts one home. It is a natural enthusiasm, not staged for the benefit of golfing etiquette.

"He's good," says caddie Leonard Thomas, "except when he starts hooking. Then he plays bad. He's got a lot of nerve, though."

"Nerve—that's what keeps coming up about Lanny," says veteran Dave Marr. "I think it's probably premature to say he's the best ball striker around, as some people have, but there's no doubt he's good. He's criticized for his grip and his swing, but there must be something right about them. They work under pressure."

Compared to the perfection of a Nicklaus, any newcomer will be given the once-over when it comes time to tee up the ball. Wadkins is no exception. He even admits he doesn't fully understand his own swing.

"I was taught the basics and then just told to whomp it. I haven't sought any advice. I was playing well enough that I didn't want to mess around with anything. But you can learn a lot by just watching. I watch the good ball strikers—Nicklaus, Weiskopf, Knudson, Aaron, Snead, Heard—

Johnny Miller, 25, almost pulled eye-opening upset in 1971 Masters.

Despite withered left arm, Larry Hinson is one of tour's top youngsters.

to make myself aware of the things they all do well: takeaway, shoulder turn, leg action. Putting is the weakest part of my game and I'm going to have to work on that."

One pro theorizes that Wadkins' putting isn't weak, that it's just overshadowed by the rest of his game. Lanny had taken to whistling on the greens, however, in an effort to soothe himself during the pressure moments.

"Sometimes it just relaxes you a little. It's good to be easy-going and carefree. I guess I've learned that from playing practice rounds with Jerry Heard."

Both young men share a rented home in California. Heard, who is in his fourth year on the tour, also won over $100,000 in 1972. "Lanny has some things to learn," he says, "just like we all do—things having to do with attitude. He tends to get mad at himself, to let things upset him once in a while. But he has so much ability that I don't see any reason why he shouldn't be great."

Wadkins is married and so the chances that he will slip in the ensuing years may be reduced. Many of the youngsters who broke in big (Murphy for one) had difficulty the second year. But with his wife as a stabilizing influence, Lanny should continue to win big.

"Lanny is going to earn more money than he can count in the next ten years," says Bert Yancey. "He's already a star. There is only one question: is he going to be like a Palmer, Player or Nicklaus?"

Wadkins, uncharacteristically, speaks with more restraint about his second year. "For a start, I'll try to win a tournament again, and as soon as possible. Beyond that, I haven't thought very much about it. Maybe there is such a thing as a sophomore slump. I don't know. But I don't intend to find out. It seems to me that if you're good, you're going to play good consistently."

Though the travel is enjoyable at first, Lanny and his wife lost a bit of their youthful drive during the long summer months. "There were some bad towns," Lanny said. "But there were some good times and it's fun to go back to a tournament you've played well in. It sparks you up to have people shouting encouragement to you."

Wadkins will find that kind of greeting when the next Sahara Invitational is held. It represents his first tour victory and he had to beat out Palmer and Nicklaus to win it. He fired a 273—11 under par on the 6,800 Sahara Nevada Country Club course. Lanny shot a 69 the final day, a round that was matched by Palmer. Lanny had to struggle at first, but he sank a six-foot birdie putt on the ninth hole to move ahead for good. It was an especially frustrating defeat for Palmer, who finished the year without a tournament victory. "I've had a lot of disappointments in golf and I've had a lot of fun." Turning to Wadkins, he added, "I may still be playing when he retires."

That remains to be seen. Wadkins is not going to wear himself out in the future as he did his first year when it was important to play as many tournaments as possible. He will take a couple of weeks off now and then to rest up and put his clubs aside. Golf is a year-round sport and only those who are struggling to pay their expenses must play every week. At 23, it doesn't appear as if Wadkins will have those worries again.

"It's hard to say whether Lanny will be a great player," Murphy said. "That depends on what tournaments he wins. A great player has to win major tournaments. But there's no doubt he'll win. He has that quality. You've got to remember, though, that a lot of great players had less auspicious starts than Lanny Wadkins did."

So far, it's been almost perfect for Wadkins—perhaps the most perfect start of any golfer's pro career. Will there be adversity ahead, or will Wadkins continue to improve? All the great golfers—

Young foreign players are challenging Gary Player's role, too.

Nicklaus and Palmer included—have had their slumps and their periods of doubt. They've had the dry spells that started with no explanation and ended the same way. At 23, no one is ready to tell Lanny Wadkins he's washed up even if he doesn't win $100,000. Most expect him to be earning closer to $200,000 before very long.

Wadkins' good friend, Jerry Heard, has reached the same pinnacle of success although it took him three years of trying. Heard earned over $137,000 in 1972 and, inflation or not, that's a lot of money for a 25-year-old. Jerry won the Florida Citrus and the Colonial National Invitational in Fort Worth, Texas. The victory in the Colonial was doubly important since the Citrus championship came early in the year when many of the big names of golf were just starting to put their games together. The Citrus proved to Heard he could play with the best of them.

"In my first year (1969), I studied the other golfers, and I've patterned my game after some of them. I use Dave Stockton's grip, George Archer's stroke and Bob Charles' set ups," he explains.

Heard won just $10,236 in his first year as he made the difficult transition to the constant travel and pressure of playing against the best. Yet he remained calm, confident and easy going, not allowing the pressure to get the best of him. When he gets on a golf course, though, there is little of the flamboyance that marks Lee Trevino or even Wadkins. He's all business.

"Finances, that's the difference," he says. "If Arnie or Jack comes to the last hole near the lead or in the lead, he can hit it to the pin. I use to worry about missing a shot; the difference would be as much as $10,000. I worried too much about it. It was a losing deal with my backers and I had to get out of it. Now, everything I make I keep."

Though only 25, Heard seems to be one of the more level-headed of the young pros. He's one of the best, too.

It was in the 1970 Westchester Classic that Johnny Miller first made an impression on the golfing world. He literally made a splash too. A sudden rainstorm struck the Westchester course as the final foursomes were finishing up. When the rain struck Miller ran for cover. As the brief storm subsided, he emerged with his putter and a new outfit. He had donned a baggy, green plastic rainsuit which covered his flashy peppermint striped slacks and bright blue shirt. It couldn't conceal his enthusiasm, however.

When the blond haired Miller finally made it to the clubhouse, he brought the distinction of being the last player off the course. He also had the lead—the sixth golfer to hold that position during the day. To say the least, he was unaccustomed to the lofty surroundings.

"It doesn't bother me," he said then. "I really don't expect to be here and no one else does, either.

Chi Chi Rodriguez (r) came back strong in 1972 to win $113,000.

Everybody figures we'll choke eventually."

Candid, yes, but not any more so than other young players on the tour. Miller was enjoying his celebrity status for one day, knowing he probably wouldn't be able to hold his lead against the likes of Palmer, Nicklaus, Frank Beard or the eventual winner, Bruce Crampton. He worried about being late for a dinner engagement because of the rain delay, and he asked those around him if any of them could give him a lift.

No expensive cars then for Miller, no one waiting to cater to his every need and wish. It was a strange Westchester tournament that year. Though it offered a first place prize of $50,000, many of the veteran pros griped about assorted things and Lee Trevino even missed his starting time and was disqualified. Miller seemed happy merely to be there. And true to his own prediction, he faltered in the final two rounds and was not in contention. Today, though, hardly a tournament passes when he isn't a threat to win.

Miller won over $99,000 in 1972 and was still his exuberant self. The 25-year-old native of San Francisco is in his fourth year on the tour and has earned more than $60,000 in his first two years. He won the Southern Open in 1972, but his fondest memory is the Masters he almost won in 1971.

Johnny was on the 16th hole of the final round at Augusta and well within range of the top.

Brightest of young foreign players is handsome Tony Jacklin.

However, he admitted to losing concentration and allowing his mind to wander. "I wonder how the green coat will look on me," he thought to himself. "Gee, Dad sure will love it."

The lapse in concentration was costly. Miller caught a trap with one shot on the 16th and wound up with a bogey. At the 19th, he hooked his drive, missed the green and bogeyed again. "I should have known from past history how the last couple of holes might go," he moaned. "But for 14 holes I was six under par and going like crazy. I was in so positive a mood I kept walking along telling myself this is just a practice round, so go on and keep making birdies."

After the disastrous finishing holes, Miller finished second behind Charles Coody and tied for the runner-up spot with Nicklaus. "The momentum changed after the 16th," Miller recalls. "All of a sudden, instead of thinking birdie all the time, I was thinking 'make par.' Then, at the 18th, wrong things kept running through my head. I guess I need a lot more experience. I was happy just to be there and I knew how Nicklaus must have felt about finishing second. But, believe me, I didn't feel too bad. I wasn't at all disappointed."

Matching Miller, blond hair for blond hair, and enthusiasm for enthusiasm, is Larry Hinson, a 27-year-old look-alike who slumped in 1972 after several successful years. But Hinson, who broke in on the tour in 1968 and won $4,000, is young enough to rebound and match his 1970 winnings of $120,000 in the near future. Larry won $48,000 in 1972, so it couldn't be considered a total failure. But the skinny 6-2, 150-pounder is capable of being a consistent top ten player despite the lingering effects of polio, which left one of his arms withered.

Australia's Bruce Devlin was consistent winner on 1972 PGA tour.

Larry is a native of North Carolina and now makes his home in Georgia. As a child the bout with polio paralyzed his left arm. A dedicated program of conditioning and therapy allowed him to overcome the handicap and become a successful tour player—one who can drive surprising distances for his lack of size.

"I broke my left arm three times and my right arm twice," he laughs. "I was trying to prove I was going to be an average boy despite the polio. I had some trouble convincing my parents of that, however. I decided that polio wasn't going to ruin my life. After I was better, I remember being so self-conscious about my arm that I wore a jacket all the time so no one could see it.

"Then, slowly, I decided I should play games with the rest of the guys. I did, and started getting hurt, but it was worth all the trouble. I think it gave me a better appreciation of my body. I always try to stay in shape, and even now I still squeeze those sponge balls to maintain the strength in my hands."

Hinson winds himself up like a ball on the course, to get the maximum delivery from his body off the tee. He seems to explode over the ball, following through with a flourish. In 1969, he won his first tournament when he took the New Orleans Open.

"My victory in New Orleans was something special," he says. "And it wasn't for just the money. It's important to a young golfer to get that first win. It takes the pressure off, and you realize you can play with the good golfers."

Larry Hinson may have slumped in 1972, but knowing the courage he's shown in the past, there's little doubt he'll return to the $100,000 level in the near future.

The foreign golfers on the U.S. tour have played with more and more success in recent years. In 1972, Gary Player of South Africa won over $120,000, Bruce Devlin of Australia earned $119,000, Chi-Chi Rodriguez won $113,000 and Bruce Crampton of Australia took down $111,000. Of the younger players from different parts of the world, Tony Jacklin, at 27, remains the brightest hope. He finished far down the money list with earnings of $66,000, but Jacklin is the most formidable English threat in the colonies.

Tony won the 1969 British Open by two strokes over Bob Charles and then shocked everyone, including himself, when he won the U.S. Open in 1970. "Playing the American tour has helped me immeasurably," he says. "Against this kind of competition you have to play your best every day, and doing that sharpens your game as nothing else can."

Although many thought his victory in the U.S. Open had vaulted Jacklin into a permanent place among golf's big names, Tony has had his ups and downs instead. Still, no less an authority than Arnold Palmer says, "Jacklin has the potential to be a great golfer."

Tony began to take notice of the game as a nine-year-old while caddying for his father. He competed in tournaments for boys his age and won several of them. "I knew I wanted golf to be my life," he says. "So, when I was 17, I dropped out of school and became a professional. I wouldn't recommend that to boys today, though, because I have discovered an education is an invaluable asset."

Jacklin has worked in pro

Young Jim Jamieson made break-through in winning 1972 Western Open.

shops, caddied, studied with veterans of the tour and overcome the odds of traveling 3,000 miles to a foreign country. "There is no place like the United States to learn what this game is all about," he says. "Anyone wanting to become a professional should play with these Americans. They're the best—the best to learn from."

At first glance Jim Jamieson would strike most people as a young weekend golfer who works as an accountant, banker or school teacher. But golfer? Jim Jamieson, even in a sport in which the only contact is between the club head and ball, does not look like an athlete. He is a chunky, colorful, relative newcomer who suddenly vaulted near the top of

Veteran pros give Jerry Heard great chance of reaching the top.

the money list in 1972. Most of his earlier years were ones of lucrative mediocrity. He earned nearly $40,000 consistently, but never showed the promise of becoming a threat to golfing's elite. He became such a threat in 1972 when he won $109,000.

"I probably didn't set enough goals," says the 29-year-old from Moline, Illinois. "I want to be a consistent money-winner and make a name for myself in golf, because I want to be a club professional some day."

Jamieson's biggest hurdle was cleared in 1972 when he won his first tournament—the Western Open in mid-June. He is unassuming and he hasn't let success spoil him. People delight in the way he still addresses officials as "Mr."

Jim won $31,000 in 1970—his second year on the tour—and gained enough points to make the top 60 for exemption. "I decided after that year that if I could win another $10,000 or so in 1971, I would be doing all right," he says. Jamieson earned $40,000 that next year, but the purses were bigger and he failed to make the top 60. It meant going through the process of qualifying on Mondays again, and Jim and his wife decided to drop their sponsors and try it on their own.

"We went to the West Coast for the Glen Campbell-Los Angeles Open with $4,300," he said. "I won some money, but the tournament cost us $1,000. I didn't do anything at the Crosby but then I won a little over $3,000 in Tucson and we were on our way."

Jamieson played well through the winter tour and finished second in the Florida Citrus Open. "My big break came in the Masters," he said. "Even though I had a bad last round of 77, I received a lot of exposure and confidence." He finished in a tie for fifth.

"No matter how successful a golfer might be without winning a tournament, winning the first one is still the most important step," says Jim. "When you are playing well, you get chances to win. But until you have won, it's a big hurdle to clear. Now that I've won the first one, it really doesn't seem to be that big. It will help the next time I get in position, because I know what it feels like."

The hero worship that young players accord the veterans in pro sports, has its place in golf too. But players are breaking in at such a young age that sometimes the hero is a man still in his prime. It's that way with Jack Lewis Jr., a 25-year-old pro who didn't even make the top 100 money winners in 1972. Even among the "rabbits," he is an unknown. To Lewis though, there is no one better than Arnold Palmer.

Lewis is from South Carolina and he mimicks Palmer to the point that he carries a golf glove in his hip pocket, just like Arnie, and stops to watch planes pass overhead, just like Arnie. He walks down the fairway like Arnie, wears granny glasses just like Arnie and makes facial contortions just like Arnie. The only thing he can't do is play just like Arnie.

Finally, in the summer of 1972, Jack Lewis played a few rounds of golf with Arnie. When

Arnie Palmer gave young Jack Lewis, Jr., helping hand in 1972.

Jack Nicklaus suffered an infected finger and had to withdraw from the National Team Championship at Palmer's home course at Laurel Valley, Pa., Arnie had to find a new partner. He and Nicklaus had made a mockery of the team championship in recent years, winning as they pleased. Palmer could have chosen any number of replacements, but instead he selected Lewis.

Palmer obviously wasn't concerned with winning the tournament again. Instead, he became Lewis' tutor. For Lewis, it was a dream come true.

The tournament is a best-ball competition, and the galleries at Laurel Valley hero worship Palmer as much as Lewis does. They wanted to watch Palmer as much as Lewis does. They wanted to watch Palmer and Nicklaus gun for birdies. Instead they saw golf's version of "Room 222."

"Oh, I don't know. I think people will come out to see who Jack Lewis is," Palmer said.

For Lewis it was quite an

experience. One reporter asked him if he planned to turn pro and Lewis answered, "I've been one for a couple of years." He was asked countless times if he was nervous and he answered countless times, "Well, yes, a little nervous, but I'm more fired up than nervous."

Lewis shunned the opportunity to stay at Palmer's house and stayed with some friends in nearby Johnstown. When Arnie was asked why he had chosen Lewis, he said it was because they were friends and because Jack was the first recipient of the Buddy Worsham Scholarship that Palmer established at Wake Forest in memory of a friend killed in an auto accident.

But the feeling was that Palmer had followed the career of Lewis closely and had seen how this one-time college star had slumped to the very bottom as a pro. Jack was an example of the struggles a golfer endures—and proof that not every youngster is as lucky or as good as Lanny Wadkins. Palmer was out to rescue a "rabbit."

Lewis had won just $1,400 that year after showing a great deal of promise three years earlier as a rookie. He began playing golf at six, and his parents took note of his rare ability. They offered him $1,000 if he didn't drink or smoke until his 21st birthday. The day after that milestone birthday he called his mother and said, "Well, I'm 21." She told him to go out and have some champagne.

There has been little champagne for Lewis since. It didn't appear that way, however, when he won $30,000 in prize money his first two years. "Then I started worrying about my swing," he says. "I got too analytical. And then I began pressing. Any golfer's going to hit bad shots, but I couldn't forgive mine. I lost my concentration and I lost my confidence."

That's where Palmer came in. Arnie hoped the publicity would help Lewis in the Team Championship instead of adding extra pressure. "He's young and strong," Arnie said, "and he can carry an old man."

But Palmer knew he wouldn't be winning the title in 1972. "Wrong club," he would say quietly to Lewis, or "close up that stance . . . firm up those wrists." After one round Lewis told Palmer he was going out to practice.

"Well, if you're going to practice, go out and beat the ball at something," he said. "Don't just hit it. Have a target. Firm up those wrists. You were coming off the ball and if you keep doing that, you're going to spin your wheels."

When the tournament ended, Arnie and Jack Lewis were tied for 29th place. But Lewis was confident Palmer's instruction course was going to help in the future. There are probably a lot of young pros who envied his chance to play with Palmer. The "rabbits" may be moving in on the veterans, but there are still many whose dream of being a golf pro can easily go up in smoke. For every $100,000 winner, there are a dozen who can't even make expenses. This is the bitter fact of life on the pro tour. ■

WOMEN'S GOLF

A NEW LOOK FOR THE LADY PROS

■ For all those years ladies' golf was—well, it was just ladies' golf. Most folks felt the gals should have been at home practicing their Vardon grip on the handle of a dust mop, or maybe driving the small-fry to school instead of driving a golf ball off the first tee.

The distaff golf tour was very much in evidence, but at times it seemed as if a majority of the sporting public was trying its best to forget this fact.

Besides, there was no way the ladies could compete with the men pros. How could anyone get excited over Mickey Wright when Jack Nicklaus was bidding for the

Tall, mini-skirted Carol Mann shows winning form out of sand trap.

Kathy Whitworth has been one of perennial winners on ladies' tour.

fabled Grand Slam? Which of the gals was capable of mounting an electrifying charge, as Arnold Palmer did so often? And certainly none of the women pros could match humorous one-liners with Lee Trevino.

While men's golf had made strides with the influx of a host of new, fresh-faced youngsters, the ladies' results always sounded the same. Kathy Whitworth would win, or sometimes it would be Carol Mann. Mickey Wright would be up there, and so would Sandra Haynie. It was a tired, familiar script.

But all this changed in 1972—and not because the Ladies Professional Golfers Association made home economics a required subject at the new school it is opening to screen prospective fugitives from the kitchen. All that ladies' golf really needed was a scandal, a good old-fashioned quarrel between females, something the public could relate to, something to make the lady pros appear more human, not just a bunch of wind-up dolls that play golf.

It happened in June when the LPGA abruptly suspended Jane Blalock, a long-legged 26-year-old who was the leading money-winner on the tour. The LPGA decided she had earned this distinction by cheating.

Though the charges were never really spelled out, the LPGA accused the blonde Miss Blalock of improving the greens that stood between her ball and the cup, and of occasionally moving the ball itself. Some lady golfers sneered and murmured, "No wonder she was voted the Most Improved Golfer two years in a row." The suspension, said the LPGA, would last a year.

But if the LPGA thought Jane Blalock would take her suspension sitting on her putter, the organization learned differently a week later. Miss Blalock was not ready for the kitchen—not yet. She filed a $5,000,000 anti-trust suit against the LPGA and that left it up to the U.S. District Court in Atlanta to decide her fate. Who cares about Jack Nicklaus now?

The first public reaction was that the LPGA had been too severe with its punishment. Yet golf thrives on the iron-clad inflexibility of its rules, and what would the game deteriorate to if people were allowed to place the

In 1961, Mickey Wright swept all three of the major titles on gals' tour.

ball wherever they wanted to after a poor shot? It's a sport in which Masters tournament was lost by Roberto De Vicenzo because he signed an incorrect scorecard. Not one that improved his score—but one that cost him a stroke. Such is the nature of golf.

Miss Blalock's troubles started in May at the Bluegrass Invitational in Louisville. A five-member ruling board (made up of women) called Jane in and told her she was being disqualified from the tournament because she was observed moving her ball illegally on a green. She was also fined $500.

After the Lady Carling Open a few weeks later, the LPGA announced the year-long suspension. Miss Blalock received a temporary restraining order—and the battle lines were drawn. Supposedly

Judy Rankin combines good looks and a real talent for the game of golf.

Jane had been under suspicion for over a year. Some people in the galleries claimed to have seen her moving the ball to her benefit. Jane denied everything.

Jane Blalock had never really been "one of the girls" on the tour. She never served voluntarily on a tour committee and it appeared that she wasn't overly interested in mingling socially with any of her fellow golfers. The committee which suspended her was made up of five rival pros including: Cynthia Sullivan, Judy Rankin, Penny Zavichas, Linda Craft and Sharon Miller. Miss Blalock never counted any of them as a close friend.

Jane grew up in Portsmouth, N.H., and went to college in Rollins, Florida. She wasn't much of a success with the golf clubs at Rollins, and returned home to teach. Her love for golf, though, persuaded her to give it one more try—and she headed south again. Jane was devoted to the game, more so than some of the other ladies who either envied or resented her dedicated approach to things.

"It takes a certain kind of person, and I know I wouldn't want to be *that* kind, to be able to play while all this is going on," one woman pro said. "I think Janie is *that* way."

Jane won less than $4,000 her first year on the tour, then picked up $12,000 and her first title the next year. In 1971 she jumped up to $34,000, and was ready to challenge the Whitworths and the Manns.

By June of 1972, Miss Blalock had already equaled her winnings of the previous year and had won two tournaments, including the Dinah Shore-Colgate championship in Palm Springs, Calif. The first place prize in that one was $20,000—and once that would have been looked upon as a successful year's work. Then came the suspension and few, if any, of the women golfers rushed to Jane Blalock's defense. They mostly snubbed her, talked behind her back and probably whispered that she had dishpan hands.

"I like to feel I'm a compassionate person," Jane said. "And it disturbs me to see so many other girls without compassion. During these past few weeks, I'd walk into a roomful of people and they'd stop talking when they saw me. It was like everyone knew something except me. I couldn't eat. I'd lie in bed with my eyes open. If I ever came close to losing my mind, it was then. They were playing games with a person's life. I don't think they realized it."

Armed with her court order and her clubs, Jane entered the LPGA tournament, one of the more prestigious, if not richest, events on the tour. She was followed around by the press, receiving almost as much attention as a Nicklaus or a Palmer does. She handled the pressure well, however, and finished second to Kathy Ahern, a 23-year-old newcomer to the tour. If anything, it was at least pleasing to note that a new face was collecting the winner's check—and not one of the weather-beaten standbys.

The tournament still took second to the affairs of Janie Blalock. Later the following week, Bud Erickson, executive director of the LPGA, defended the organization's actions in suspending Janie.

The Jane Blalock affair shook women's golf to foundations in 1972.

"We're not denying her a right to earn a living," he said. "She can always teach history."

"Rather than teaching history, I think I'm making some right now," was Jane's response.

Whether Jane Blalock did or

did not move a ball will probably never be resolved. It could have been something she did subconsciously, if at all. Her caddie from one tournament said he would testify in her behalf. As of now, the case is still pending. The suspension will not stick if it can't be proven conclusively that she is guilty. One way or another, the decision will put ladies' golf in the limelight again, no matter what the boys are doing.

This isn't exactly what the LPGA had in mind when it instituted a program to improve the image of women's golf and make the tour more attractive to cash customers and television producers. But it was at least a shot in the arm and maybe, in the long run, Bud Erickson and the others will thank Jane Blalock for putting the ladies' game on the front pages.

Whether she stretched the rules of the game or not, Jane Blalock is a new, refreshing and colorful personality—and this is what the LPGA desperately needs. It needs an influx of young blood, bright, pretty young gals who can swing a club and who can also breathe life and vitality into a sick women's pro tour.

The LPGA recognizes this

Penny Zavichas (left), a bright name on the gals' tour, is a niece of the late Babe Didrickson Zaharias (below).

fact—thanks, in part, to the Jane Blalock affair—and has finally set up a school for promising distaff golfers along the same lines as the men's PGA rookie school. It's a twice-a-year school that will screen applicants for the tour. A gal must have an average of 78 or lower for three 18-hole rounds. She must also pass a written exam on the rules of golf (No—Miss Blalock will not proctor this exam!) and on the LPGA's constitution and by-laws. The minimum age is 18 and players will have to finish in the upper four-fifths of the field in three of four tournaments to qualify.

Hopefully, the LPGA school will encourage potential golfers to try for a pro career. It will take time but at least it's a step in the right direction. If ladies' golf appears too establishment-oriented, it will drive the younger girls to tennis, a sport which has managed to appear fresh and new despite the fact that its tradition is more conservative than golf's.

Over the years the people who run the ladies' pro tour have never appeared overly concerned with trying to improve their public image; nor have they demonstrated any inclination to compete for popularity with the men's tour. Instead, they have been content with their own little "thing" and with re-telling the deeds of the game's few legendary players. Babe Zaharias was the first of these legends, and she was followed by other star performers such as: Patty Berg, Louise Suggs, Mickey Wright, Betsy Rawls and, more recently, Kathy Whitworth.

It might be revealing to point out that many of these "legends" are still walking the fairways on the ladies' pro tour, an indication that the game's sponsors have failed to develop a sufficient number of young players.

But perhaps it's unfair to dismiss the legends so quickly . . .

One of the more memorable events in women's golf occurred in 1947, when Babe Zaharias won the British Women's Open, the first American to accomplish the feat. Louise Suggs caught everyone's attention in 1952 when she set a U.S. Women's Open scoring record with a total of 284. In 1959, Betsy Rawls became a one-girl dynasty, winning 10 events in a single year. In 1961 Mickey Wright completed a rare sweep of the Women's Open, the LPGA and the Titleholders championships. Then, in 1969, Miss Whitworth turned in perhaps the most remarkable achievement of all when she won four consecutive tournaments in the span of five weeks. No man had ever dominated golf as Miss Whitworth had for that one month.

When a first lady of golf is mentioned, however, it usually is Mildred Didrickson Zaharias, alias the Babe. She was born in Port Arthur, Texas, and she crammed more excitement, fun, glamour and glory into her 42 years than most people do in 70. She died in 1956 of cancer.

In 1932, Babe entered the National AAU Women's Track and Field Meet, which that year doubled as the Olympic Trials. She won five events and finished second in another. She also won an Olympic berth, and went to the Games in Los Angeles, where she took two gold medals—in the 80 meter hurdles and in the javelin throw. Babe became a national heroine. Shortly after the Olym-

pics, she turned pro for $3,500 a week and toured the country.

Babe Zaharias once pitched an inning against the Philadelphia Phillies and once struck out Joe DiMaggio. She worked out with the SMU football team, won a fly-casting contest and finally established herself as the single outstanding female in such sports as softball, bowling and swimming. She hadn't even discovered golf at that time.

"I want to be the best woman golfer in the world," she once said. Then she made her professional debut. It was the first time she had ever swung a club. And at the Brentwood Country Club in Santa Monica, California, she shot a nine-hole total of 43. Babe was a strong driver, booming 250-yard shots off the tee that many of the men of the tour would have been envious of.

In 1946, Babe entered the Women's Amateur championship at the Southern Hills Country Club in Tulsa, Okla., and won. During the next two years she captured 15 tournaments, and later Babe Zaharias signed a con-

Improved play of distaff golfers is attracting larger galleries these days.

Patty Berg was a dominant figure on women's tour for many years.

Betsy Rawls has several Women's Open titles to her credit.

tract to do movie shorts for $300,000. When she died in 1956, the golf world mourned. She was the first super-star among female athletes and she had helped spark interest in women's sports.

Mickey Wright inherited the crown after Babe's death and has worn it well. She has won over 80 professional tournaments and is still active today, a veteran at 37 and an original member of the Women's Golf Hall of Fame. In 1958, her fourth year on the tour, Mickey won her first two major titles, the LPGA and the Women's Open. She holds the record for most birdies shot in an 18-hole round, with nine. In 1963, she so dominated the sport that she won 13 of the 28 official tournaments, breaking Betsy Rawls' record.

Mickey Wright was as dominant in her time as Babe Zaharias had been in hers. But she was flattered when anyone compared her to the Babe. "I don't think that's fair," she said. "Mrs. Zaharias was in a class by herself. As for me, I prefer just being Mickey Wright, and I want to be the best woman golfer in the world."

Louise Suggs and Patty Berg shared some of the spotlight prior to the start of the Mickey Wright era. Patty won the first Women's Open in 1946 and won 83 tournaments overall. She had seven Titleholders championships to her credit, as well as seven Western Opens and four World Championships. Patty was the leading money-winner in 1954, 1955 and 1957.

Babe Zaharias, Patty Berg and

Kathy Whitworth (kneeling) is one of top putters among women pros.

5

JoAnne Carner, five-time U.S. Amateur champion and one of the longest hitters on the women's pro tour today, travels to all LPGA tournaments in a modern trailer home with her husband, Don. Although purses on the LPGA tour are getting bigger every year, most gals still must find a way to keep expenses to a minimum. Without a trailer home such as this, JoAnne might spend as much as $20,000 a year on such items as hotels, meals, air travel—and that wouldn't include hubby Don.

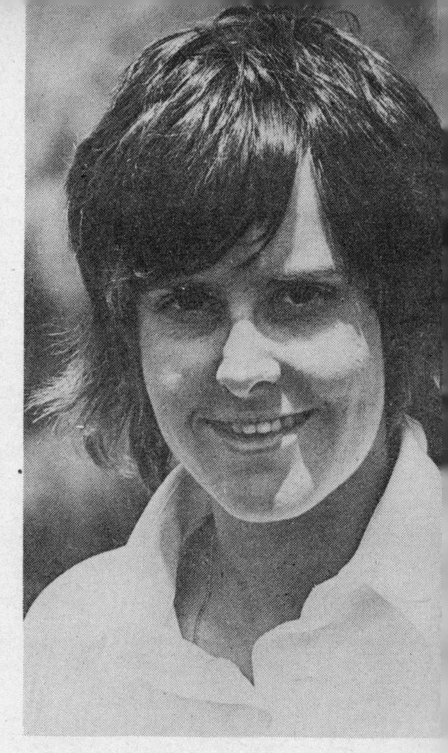

some of the other "pioneers" probably wouldn't recognize the women's tour today. The gals are better players, the scores are much lower and, best of all, the purses are much bigger. Then, too, increased television coverage has thrown more of a public spotlight on skilled players like Kathy Whitworth who, in time, might prove to be better than all of them.

In 1960, after only two years on the tour, Kathy won the Most Improved Player Award. She captured it the next year, too, after winning three tournaments, including the Open. In 1962, she won eight tournaments. Kathy slumped to one victory in 1964, but the following year she vaulted to the top again, winning eight tournaments, $28,000 and the Associated Press designation as Women Athlete of the Year.

Once a woman begins to dominate, she usually remains at the top for several years. This was true with the Babe and Mickey Wright and it is true with Kathy Whitworth today. In 1968 she won 11 tournaments and was named Pro Player of the Year. She earned over $48,000 in the process. And while she didn't win as much the following year, 1969 proved to be the most consistent for her. Kathy entered 28 tourneys and finished in the top ten in 27. She won seven, including those four straight in a five-week span. It started with the Orange Blossom Open in St. Petersburg, Fla., on March 13. She then won the Port Charlotte Invitational, the Port Malabar Invitational and topped off her hot streak with a victory in the Lady Carling Open, in Palmetto.

"I admire Mickey Wright for her superior skills," said Carol Mann, a tour regular. "But Kathy has great inner strength. She is probably a better competitor because she had to be. She is the best under pressure of anybody who ever played on this tour."

The ladies insist that Kathy never three-putts, that she doesn't make mistakes around the greens. They consider her a magician of sorts. "When she has to putt, I mean absolutely has to make it for a victory, she gets it every time," Sandra Haynie says. "Post and I tied at Port Charlotte in 1969 and Kathy needed a seven-footer to beat us. I put on my bracelets and was ready to go home before she hit the ball. There wasn't going to be a playoff."

The success of Kathy Whitworth and Carol Mann in recent years has helped create at least a handful of new young pros who may share the wealth a bit more in the future than the ladies have been doing in the past. Sandra Post, JoAnne Gunderson Carner, Clifford Ann Creed, Shirley Englehorn, Susie Berning, Judy Rankin, Kathy Ahern, Debbie Austin, Pam Barnett and Margie Masters are among the newcomers.

"For the women, the secret will be in their irons and their approach shots," said one male

The new—and pretty—look on gals' tour includes (clockwise from top left) Kathy Ahern, Pam Barnett, Susie Berning and Clifford Ann Creed.

pro. "Maybe they can't match the men in strength off the tee, but there is no reason why they can't match them in chipping and putting. Driving 250 yards is not really necessary if the irons are good. Look at some of the less rugged men players, such as Gary Player. He was never a long hitter, but his game on the fairways is second to none."

But if the American gals think they will have the purses all to themselves in the U.S., they have another thought coming. In the summer of 1972, the Japanese sent four women golfers to the U.S. to compete on the LPGA tour. It did not come as a shock, since the Japanese have made several inroads in professional golf in recent years. They also host several tourneys of their own in which Americans compete. Today there are over 650 golf courses in Japan and the country boasts 10 million golfers.

The Japanese women, whose role in golf was usually to serve as caddies, are now becoming pros themselves. "After the war two things got stronger in Japan—nylon stockings and women," says Steve Kawaguchi, the interpreter who traveled through America with the four lady golfers. "Women's liberation isn't so well organized in Japan but there aren't many henpecked husbands there, either."

R.K. Mizuno Sporting Goods, the world's fourth largest sporting equipment company, sponsored two of the traveling girls, Chako Higuchi and Marbo Sasaki. The firm paid all the expenses and the golfers get to keep whatever they earn. It was the girls' third visit and this time they brought along two compatriots, Sayoko Yamazaki and Etsuko Nakamura. And since the Japanese are small people, the play of the four representatives of Nippon should do nothing but encourage their petite American counterparts.

"They violate every rule we've been taught," says Dede Owens, an American pro. "But they're fantastic wedge players, and I think Higuchi would rather be in a trap than on the green."

The Japanese have been awed by the size of most American women golfers and also by the fact that many U.S. gals are still competing successfully though in their 30s. "When we talk about viewing Mickey Wright from a Japanese sense, she is regarded as an old lady but she still has great power," observes Miss Sasaki.

So far, the Japanese girls haven't had much success in U.S. tournaments. But gradually the Japanese are getting to feel more at home and are learning how to get around. They are also learning to communicate with Americans and eventually the feeling of being more at ease will bring success on the course. What will happen if and when a Japanese girl wins an American tournament no one knows. It will probably start a trend in Japan with girl golfers trying to win their way to the U.S. the following year.

More young American women will also be attracted to the pro tour. It's a good life, the money is getting better and the image of the touring pro has been upgraded significantly. ■

Huge gallery encircles the first tee at Augusta during the Masters.

EVEN A LOSER CAN MAKE 50Gs ON PRO GOLF TOUR

■ A man stands hunched over a small white ball, staring at it for what seems to be the amount of time it takes a television station to break for a dog food commercial, one for deodorant and another for mouthwash. He's dressed in a pair of brightly colored slacks, a knit shirt and sometimes a cap. Even after the viewer has gargled with Listerine and brushed with Gleem, the guy is still standing there. But why not? After all, some announcer has just finished whispering to his audience that the putt the golfer is about to attempt is worth $20,000 if not more.

At one time $20,000 would have led all golfers in earnings for an entire year. And it was just a decade ago that between $40,000 and $50,000 was considered an extraordinary year's work for a professional. But how things have changed! Today a golfer can go through an entire year without winning a tournament, or even placing in the top ten, and still win close to $50,000. Those who can work their way into an occasional high finish—especially in a tournament such as the Westchester Classic—can easily earn over $100,000.

The rapid increase in golf purses can best be described by comparing it to the clearing of the 16-foot barrier in the pole vault. Once it was finally accomplished, it seemed as if everyone was vaulting over 16 feet, then 17 and now 18. Golf's phenomenal rise has been the same. Once Arnold Palmer became the first golfer to clear $100,000 for a single season, the list has gotten longer every year. And now the goals have risen even higher. From $100,000, golfers such as Jack Nicklaus and Lee Trevino, in addition to Palmer, have surpassed the $200,000 barrier. In 1972, Nicklaus had won over $320,000 by mid-December.

In fact, 1972 turned out to be the biggest year yet for everyone in professional golf. After Nicklaus, Trevino was second with more than $200,000 in prize winnings. Fourteen others, including George Archer, Grier Jones, Jerry Heard, Tom Weiskopf, Gary Player, Bruce Devlin, Tommy Aaron, Lanny Wadkins, Bobby Mitchell, Hale Irwin, Bruce Crampton, Doug Sanders and Jim Jamieson, all won over $100,000. Several others, Dave Hill, Johnny Miller, Homero Blancas and Lou Graham among them, earned over $90,000.

And while many golf fans felt sorry for the aging Arnold Palmer and expressed concern over his inability to win, how many people can earn more than $80,000 when they're "over the hill?" Palmer, for one.

Many of the big money winners are newcomers to the tour. This isn't surprising. A whole generation of kids watching golf at home on TV are grabbing drivers and sand wedges in numbers as great as those who still prefer football and baseball. Colleges offer more scholarships and golfers such as Palmer have grants in their names awarded at major universities. The lure of the pro golf tour and the opportunity to win substantial amounts of money in a short period of time are difficult to ignore for a teenager with athletic ability.

There aren't many people, even avid golf fans, who have heard of players such as John Schlee, Jerry McGee and Chuck Courtney. Yet all earned over $50,000 in 1972. Nor is the rise in golf purses confined to the U.S. Japan has the world's richest tournament—a $300,000 event held in October of 1972 for the first time. The winner's share came to $60,000,

George Archer, a great putter, was in group over $100,000 in 1972.

3 3 2 2 2
3 3 3 2

surpassing the $50,000 offered to the winner of the Westchester Classic. In Japan alone, prize money has risen from $270,000 to $1,015,000 in three years. The PGA tour is worth $7,500,000.

Much of the increase in golf's popuarlity and purse money is directly tied to television. It brought the sport into the homes of people who had always believed golf was only a rich man's game. While golf is not always the most exciting event to watch, it served to introduced the working man to a new way of spending leisure time. Though many could not afford the membership fee of expensive country clubs, the public courses were available and most often were jammed with weekend golfers.

The golf "madness" starts in January when the tour's new year opens. The tournaments are held on the West Coast or in Florida and viewers at home (still snowed in for another two or three months) watch with envy as players in short sleeves walk 18 holes on emaculately kept courses bordered by swaying palm trees.

Celebrities have also helped increase the interest and prize winnings. Jackie Gleason, Bob Hope, Andy Williams, and the most famous show business golfer of them all, Bing Crosby, lend their names to tournaments. In some of these events, the first two rounds are pro-ams, with the professionals taking on an amateur playing partner, one often a well-known motion picture or television star. It has helped draw a type of viewer who may not have the slightest interest in golf, but who wants to see his or her favorite personality.

The players themselves provide color. Chi-Chi Rodriguez, Doug Sanders and Lee Trevino have become three of the more colorful performers on the tour, and of course Palmer's own special kind of magic and his magnificent ability to come from behind make him a natural with the galleries.

Still, because of the relatively slow pace of the game and a lack of sustained action, golf has come up for an occasional re-evaluation

Big tourney purses have made Gary Player a wealthy young man.

by TV network executives. In the summer of 1970, there was a rumor that coverage would be reduced in the ensuing years because of a tight money market and a general lack of interest. Another report was that golf had reached its saturation point on television.

At that time, Joseph Dey, commissioner of the Professional Golfers Association Tournament Players Division, assured the public that there would be no reduction in TV exposure.

The major networks televise an average of between 20 and 25 tournaments a year. Aside from the glamorous U.S. and British Opens, and the PGA and Masters, most of the interest from viewers comes during the early part of the year, when the football season has ended and before the start of baseball. Basketball and hockey games are televised during the early afternoon, while the golf tournaments from the West Coast don't appear on the home screens in the higher population areas of the East until 4 or 5 P.M.

The economic recession of the late 1960s and into the 1970s also caused independent operators such as the Hughes Sports Network to drop some of their golf coverage. "The ratings have been fairly consistent but the sales response to golf has not been as strong as before," a spokesman said. "Because of the present state of the economy, we simply felt we may have to reduce our golf program."

While television did introduce many people to golf, the sport is not geared to keep a fan glued to

Young Jim Jamieson is already in the six-figure bracket on PGA tour.

his seat watching even a Nicklaus or a Palmer battle out of the rough. Thus, the PGA has taken steps to make golf a more entertaining spectator sport. Faster playing rounds are the object of the tour leaders. Nicklaus, for example, is one of the slowest golfers on the tour and on occasion grumbling of one form or another can be heard from his fellow pros. Speeding up play has become a "must." In 1970 commissioner Dey instituted an experiment which was designed to create more interest for the spectators, make it easier for golfers to be identified on television, eliminate much of the "housekeeping" around the greens and increase the tempo of the game. He grouped players in pairs, instead of in threes and fours. Although officials and players complain of prolonged five-hour rounds, there has been a general reluctance to impose the two-stroke penalty for delay. They feel it would be unfair to deprive a golfer of winning a tournament just because of slow play.

The two-man pairing system followed the same pattern used on the tour in the Masters, British and U.S. Opens, the tournaments with the highest viewing audiences. Statistics over a three-year period revealed that four hours and 22 minutes were needed for threesomes to play a round. When the pairings were in twos for the third and fourth rounds, only three hours and 34 minutes were needed.

"We feel golfers alone among athletes are required to compete continuously for up to four hours," Dey says. "If our present experiment succeeds, we believe our fans will see a better show and the competition also will be keener."

Money also has changed another aspect of golf—the weekly Monday qualifying rounds. There are 15 categories by which a golfer may move into a starting field without participating in the Monday qualifying test. They include: exemptions for former PGA and U.S. Open champions, the low 24 scorers in the PGA championship, those who survive the 36-hole cut in the previous week's tournament and the 60 leading money winners from the previous year.

Al Balding, a veteran pro from Toronto, would change that system. He would substitute a point system to replace the money-winning exemption.

"I think a method that would allocate credits for performances would be fairer than just using the money-winning as a basis," he states. "Nowadays, if you are second twice in a big-money tournament, you can be exempt from a whole year's qualifying."

Jerry Heard uses body 'English' to help birdie putt into the cup.

In 1968, a golfer in 60th place won $28,382. In 1972, a relative unknown named Bob E. Smith held down 60th place well into December with earnings of $43,297. It has become apparent that anyone who manages to finish second, third or fourth in a major tournament such as the Westchester Classic could stumble through the rest of the year, barely making the cut, and still be exempt from weekly qualifying. Such is the effect of the increased purses.

But Balding's complaint was a mere whisper compared to the

controversy that almost cost golf severely in the summer of 1968. With millions of dollars on the line and hundreds of promoters and players involved, the sport suffered through its first serious break between the PGA and a new group, the American Professional Golfers.

At the time, representatives of both groups said money wasn't the reason for the split. Warren Orlick, then treasurer of the PGA, said his association "does not depend nor never has depended on television or the tournament program for its existence."

The PGA is broken down into profit and non-profit divisions. Income from the tour goes into a taxable fund. Dues-paying members contribute to the operation of the non-profit sector. According to Orlick, there were 6,295 members at the time, including resident country club pros and regulars on the playing tour. Over 4,000 of those paid dues of $65.00 annually as Class A members. The remainder—assistants at clubs, those who work at driving ranges and unemployed golfers—pay as little as $17.50 annually. Those who enter tournaments each week must pay the PGA an entry fee of $50.00 and it's estimated over $350,000 is raised each year by this method.

If tournaments are classed as "invitational," then the entry fee is paid by the sponsors to the PGA. The PGA also receives royalties from the sale of golf equipment bearing its name. This amounts to well over $100,000 a year. The income from television coverage of the PGA champion-

Johnny Miller is among top wage-earners on the annual pro golf trail.

ship gives that organization several hundred thousand dollars of added revenue. It's a thriving organization.

Yet the playing pros rebelled in 1968, even though the PGA had helped increase the prize money for them. The golfers said they appreciated the money, but they wanted more say in the running of tournaments and in the rules that affected them. "No one has ever suggested that the PGA was running away with the money," one pro said.

"All the players asked," said Sam Gates, attorney for the American Professional Golfers, "is the right within the PGA to work out the practical rules under which they, not the PGA officials, must play in these tournaments. They have asked the right to cast the deciding vote on matters which primarily affect them."

The rift between the players and the PGA brought the sport its first taste of bad publicity. The public does not react favorably most of the time to athletes griping—about money or most other matters. The public views pro athletes as fortunate people who live ideal lives, glamorous, profitable and enjoyable.

Threatened strikes by professionals in most sports were becoming vogue then, but it seemed strange that golf, looked upon as a gentleman's game, should be in the forefront. But whether the pros wanted to admit it or not, the sudden increase in prize winnings did play a part in the rift with the PGA. Everyone realized the golf boom of the late 1960s would not last forever, so both sides were attempting to make as much as possible while the financial tide was at its crest.

But money matters and TV ratings were the farthest thing from anyone's mind in 1972 when the bid for a Grand Slam by Jack Nicklaus brought the most complete coverage of any tournament in history. When Nicklaus won the U.S. Open at Pebble Beach, NBC used more cameras and cable equipment than ever before to bring viewers action from the holes they had only read about in the past. To those who learned their golf watching television, the 14th, 15th, 16th, 17th and 18th holes seemed to be the only ones a golfer played. The rest were myths, obviously created by an imaginative producer.

In 1972, however, NBC picked up the golfers as they turned the front nine and captured all the scenic beauty of Pebble Beach. With Palmer and Lee Trevino making a run at Nicklaus that final day, the event emerged as one of the best television sports attractions of the season. When Nicklaus won, it guaranteed an unprecedented television audience for the British Open.

As 1972 ended, Nicklaus had failed for his Grand Slam but, as already mentioned, he had won over $300,000. When will the purses level off? It's anyone's guess. Winning today is not the important thing in golf; making the cut is. A player who can finish each tournament and occasionally be among the winners can anticipate a profitable career. All he actually has to do is show up each week along the pro tour. ■